DISCRIMINATION

OPPOSING VIEWPOINTS®

OTHER BOOKS OF RELATED INTEREST

OPPOSING VIEWPOINTS SERIES

An Aging Population
AIDS
American Values
America's Prisons
America's Victims
Censorship
Civil Liberties
The Death Penalty
Feminism
Gangs
The Homeless
Homosexuality

Illegal Immigration
Interracial America
Islam
Juvenile Crime
Male/Female Roles
Mental Illness
Poverty
Race Relations
Social Justice
Violence
Welfare

CURRENT CONTROVERSIES SERIES

The Disabled
Gay Rights
Genetics and Intelligence
Hate Crimes

Illegal Immigration
Nationalism and Ethnic Conflict
Violence Against Women
Women in the Military

AT ISSUE SERIES

Affirmative Action
Environmental Justice
Ethnic Conflict
Immigration Policy
The Jury System

Single-Parent Families
The Spread of AIDS
Welfare Reform
What Is Sexual Harassment?

DISCRIMINATION

OPPOSING VIEWPOINTS®

David L. Bender, *Publisher*
Bruno Leone, *Executive Editor*
Scott Barbour, *Managing Editor*
Brenda Stalcup, *Senior Editor*
Mary E. Williams, *Book Editor*

OPPOSING
VIEWPOINTS®
SERIES

Greenhaven Press, Inc., San Diego, California

Library of Congress Cataloging-in-Publication Data

Discrimination : opposing viewpoints / Mary E. Williams, book editor.
    p.   cm. — (Opposing viewpoints series)
    Includes bibliographical references and index.
    ISBN 1-56510-657-1 (alk. paper). —
ISBN 1-56510-656-3 (pbk. : alk. paper)
    1. Discrimination—United States. 2. Minorities—United States.
3. Reverse discrimination—United States. I. Williams, Mary E.,
1960– . II. Series: Opposing viewpoints series (Unnumbered)
JC599.U5D57 1997
305.8'00973—dc21   96-49920
                                                  CIP

Every effort has been made to trace the owners of copyrighted material.

Greenhaven Press, Inc., P.O. Box 289009
San Diego, CA 92198-9009

"CONGRESS SHALL MAKE NO LAW. . . ABRIDGING THE FREEDOM OF SPEECH, OR OF THE PRESS."

First Amendment to the U.S. Constitution

The basic foundation of our democracy is the First Amendment guarantee of freedom of expression. The Opposing Viewpoints Series is dedicated to the concept of this basic freedom and the idea that it is more important to practice it than to enshrine it.

CONTENTS

WHY CONSIDER OPPOSING VIEWPOINTS?

> "The only way in which a human being can make some approach to knowing the whole of a subject is by hearing what can be said about it by persons of every variety of opinion and studying all modes in which it can be looked at by every character of mind. No wise man ever acquired his wisdom in any mode but this."
>
> **John Stuart Mill**

In our media-intensive culture it is not difficult to find differing opinions. Thousands of newspapers and magazines and dozens of radio and television talk shows resound with differing points of view. The difficulty lies in deciding which opinion to agree with and which "experts" seem the most credible. The more inundated we become with differing opinions and claims, the more essential it is to hone critical reading and thinking skills to evaluate these ideas. Opposing Viewpoints books address this problem directly by presenting stimulating debates that can be used to enhance and teach these skills. The varied opinions contained in each book examine many different aspects of a single issue. While examining these conveniently edited opposing views, readers can develop critical thinking skills such as the ability to compare and contrast authors' credibility, facts, argumentation styles, use of persuasive techniques, and other stylistic tools. In short, the Opposing Viewpoints Series is an ideal way to attain the higher-level thinking and reading skills so essential in a culture of diverse and contradictory opinions.

In addition to providing a tool for critical thinking, Opposing Viewpoints books challenge readers to question their own strongly held opinions and assumptions. Most people form their opinions on the basis of upbringing, peer pressure, and personal, cultural, or professional bias. By reading carefully balanced opposing views, readers must directly confront new ideas as well as the opinions of those with whom they disagree. This is not to simplistically argue that everyone who reads opposing views will—or should—change his or her opinion. Instead, the series enhances readers' understanding of their own views by encouraging confrontation with opposing ideas. Careful examination of others' views can lead to the readers' understanding of the logical inconsistencies in their own opinions, perspective on why they hold an opinion, and the consideration of the possibility that their opinion requires further evaluation.

EVALUATING OTHER OPINIONS

To ensure that this type of examination occurs, Opposing Viewpoints books present all types of opinions. Prominent spokespeople on different sides of each issue as well as well-known professionals from many disciplines challenge the reader. An additional goal of the series is to provide a forum for other, less known, or even unpopular viewpoints. The opinion of an ordinary person who has had to make the decision to cut off life support from a terminally ill relative, for example, may be just as valuable and provide just as much insight as a medical ethicist's professional opinion. The editors have two additional purposes in including these less known views. One, the editors encourage readers to respect others' opinions—even when not enhanced by professional credibility. It is only by reading or listening to and objectively evaluating others' ideas that one can determine whether they are worthy of consideration. Two, the inclusion of such viewpoints encourages the important critical thinking skill of objectively evaluating an author's credentials and bias. This evaluation will illuminate an author's reasons for taking a particular stance on an issue and will aid in readers' evaluation of the author's ideas.

As series editors of the Opposing Viewpoints Series, it is our hope that these books will give readers a deeper understanding of the issues debated and an appreciation of the complexity of even seemingly simple issues when good and honest people disagree. This awareness is particularly important in a democratic society such as ours in which people enter into public debate to determine the common good. Those with whom one disagrees should not be regarded as enemies but rather as people whose views deserve careful examination and may shed light on one's own.

Thomas Jefferson once said that "difference of opinion leads to inquiry, and inquiry to truth." Jefferson, a broadly educated man, argued that "if a nation expects to be ignorant and free . . . it expects what never was and never will be." As individuals and as a nation, it is imperative that we consider the opinions of others and examine them with skill and discernment. The Opposing Viewpoints Series is intended to help readers achieve this goal.

David L. Bender & Bruno Leone,
Series Editors

INTRODUCTION

"Affirmative action has always been an aberration from [America's] best principles. The time has come to end it."
—Terry Eastland

"If America ends affirmative action before addressing the underlying causes of inequality of opportunity, racial divisions will deepen."
—Chang-Lin Tien

On November 5, 1996, California voters agreed to adopt the California Civil Rights Initiative (CCRI), a ballot measure designed to end affirmative action programs in government hiring, contracting, and public education. Noting the widespread support that the initiative received both in California and throughout the United States, many policymakers view the CCRI as an example that other states—and perhaps the federal government—may eventually follow. Supporters of the CCRI would likely agree with California high school senior Scott Hunter's comments on the initiative's victory: "I'm all for it. I think it's going back to the civil rights initiative of '64, which disallowed discrimination."

The Civil Rights Act of 1964, which prohibited job discrimination based on age, race, religion, gender, or national origin, provided the groundwork for affirmative action policies. As early as 1965, these policies were implemented to correct the effects of discrimination on women and minorities by requiring employers to take "affirmative" measures to achieve gender and ethnic diversity in the workplace. Such measures typically include aggressive recruitment techniques and outreach programs designed to enlarge the pool of qualified female and minority job applicants. According to the Equal Employment Opportunity Commission, affirmative action "is considered essential to assuring that jobs are genuinely and equally accessible to qualified persons, without regard to their sex, racial, or ethnic characteristics."

Many critics of affirmative action policies, however, argue that such measures are no longer necessary because blatant racial discrimination and intolerance have been adequately brought under control. Glynn Custred, one of the authors of the CCRI, contends that "the feelings about race now in the 1990s are really quite different than they were in the 1950s. In fact, we don't give ourselves enough credit for this, but it's a massive job of [antidiscriminatory] education we've done over these past thirty years. The situation today of acceptance is different than it was then, and therefore you need different methods to assure everyone's treated equally."

Different methods are especially needed, CCRI supporters maintain, because affirmative action policies have created a system of racial and gender preferences in hiring and in education. Affirmative action critics argue that these preferences favor women and minorities simply because of group affiliation and are, in effect, a form of government-sanctioned discrimination. Such discrimination, they contend, gives privileges to some groups while placing others at a disadvantage, thereby violating the foundations of equality guaranteed in the U.S. Constitution.

Furthermore, some CCRI advocates argue that affirmative action calls attention to racial and ethnic differences and thereby creates divisiveness among groups. This divisiveness leads to increased racial tensions and interethnic conflict, they maintain. In a 1995 *USA Today* article, for example, California assemblyman Bernie Richter claims that affirmative action in its present form "creates racial hate, animosity and frustration in ways the Ku Klux Klan couldn't even invent." In addition, California governor Pete Wilson contends that affirmative action damages the ideal of American unity: "Rather than uniting people around our common core, this system of preferential treatment constantly reminds us of our superficial differences. Instead of treating every American as an individual, it pits group against group, race against race. Instead of moving us toward a color-blind society, it is holding us back." CCRI supporters conclude, therefore, that dismantling affirmative action is the best approach currently available for ending discrimination.

Critics of the CCRI, on the other hand, support affirmative action because they believe it is still the best way to create equal opportunity in employment and education for women and people of color. Although many of these critics agree with CCRI supporters that incidents of blatant discrimination have decreased since the passage of the 1964 Civil Rights Act, they contend that racism and sexism continue to limit opportunities for women and minorities. A February 1995 *San Francisco Chronicle* editorial points out that "one look at the nation's corporate and public boardrooms, which are overwhelmingly dominated by white males, should tell Americans that the country is still far from having achieved equal opportunity for all. . . . Women and people of color have not yet reached parity in government, education and myriads of other professions, especially in positions of authority." Such evidence, CCRI opponents maintain, proves that discrimination still exists in society's institutions and that affirmative action efforts should not be abandoned.

In response to CCRI advocates' argument that affirmative action policies benefit women and people of color simply because of their minority status, CCRI critics contend that white men have enjoyed privileged status because of their group affiliation for much of America's history. Women and people of color, however, have been and continue to be systematically denied a "fair shot" at many employment and educational opportunities merely because of their group affiliation, these critics argue. Ignoring or discounting minority group affinity, they assert, does not further the cause of equal opportunity. In the opinion of San Francisco State University professor Rita Takahashi, "Judgments based on skin color, ethnicity, culture, and gender are real. Recognizing this fact, dealing with it, and rectifying injustices are what is needed to move this country forward. We need to take off the blinders, suspend denials, and stop pretending that group affinity does not count."

Many CCRI opponents also take issue with the claim that affirmative action in itself creates interethnic divisiveness and conflict. Instead, they argue, racial tensions often stem from ignorance about America's diverse, pluralistic nature. These critics maintain that when people lack knowledge about cultures, values, or belief systems other than their own, they tend to fear measures that will bring them into contact with individuals from other racial or ethnic groups. However, affirmative action supporters contend, such measures actually encourage the diversification of society by increasing the amount of interethnic contact in workplaces and educational environments. They claim that the intentional inclusion of diverse groups in society's institutions eventually decreases racial tensions and discourages discriminatory attitudes. Takahashi, for example, asserts that "through affirmative action, there is an effort . . . to bring people together, rather than to keep them apart." In the final analysis, CCRI opponents conclude, retaining affirmative action policies is the best solution to the problem of discrimination.

As the CCRI and other proposals to eliminate affirmative action policies gain support, policymakers, educators, workers, political activists, and others increasingly debate the causes of and possible solutions to discrimination. *Discrimination: Opposing Viewpoints* spotlights this ongoing controversy in the following chapters: Is Discrimination a Serious Problem? What Causes Discrimination? Are Claims of Reverse Discrimination Valid? How Can Society Put an End to Discrimination?

CHAPTER 1

IS DISCRIMINATION A SERIOUS PROBLEM?

CHAPTER PREFACE

Writing in the *Prison Mirror*, Charles Bates, a middle-aged black counselor, relates his experience of being repeatedly harassed at a public library by a white police officer who assumed Bates was a criminal simply because of his race. Bates contends that the officer did not take into account his professional appearance and his physical differences from the description of the criminal suspect he was searching for. Instead, Bates asserts, the officer saw "a stereotype of his own making."

Many civil rights advocates argue that the discriminatory attitudes that can result in incidents like the above are all too common in American society. Such discrimination, they claim, is sometimes overt and noticeable, as is the case with racially motivated name-calling and epithets. However, they maintain that many less-obvious forms of discrimination result from practices that are sanctioned by society's institutions. This "institutional discrimination," according to James Jones, author of *Prejudice and Racism*, "can be defined as those established laws, customs and practices which systematically reflect and produce racial inequalities." Despite antidiscrimination laws that advocate equitable treatment for all, civil rights advocates maintain, institutional discrimination remains an impediment to equal opportunity for African Americans.

Others disagree with the contention that discrimination is a serious problem. Black economist Thomas Sowell, for example, argues that claims of police discrimination against black men are exaggerated: "I keep reading stuff by deep thinkers . . . who tell me that every encounter between a black male and the cops is sheer hostility or humiliation. But I keep thinking back over the years to my various encounters with the police and cannot come up with examples to match theirs." In Sowell's opinion, the media's preference for stories that spotlight racial tensions creates the illusion that African Americans encounter constant discrimination. Still others, including *Wall Street Journal* staff writer Jason L. Riley, believe that blacks often blame their own inadequacies on discrimination and "raise the issue of race when it has no direct relevance." Riley contends that "in this country, such an accident of birth [being black] gives one license to raise the specter of racial prejudice whenever ill-fortune visits—invited or no."

The pervasiveness of discrimination against African Americans is just one of the issues debated in the following chapter; claims of discrimination against women, immigrants, and homosexuals are also examined.

"Poverty in the U.S. is increasingly synonymous with people of color."

DISCRIMINATION CAUSES BLACK POVERTY

Robert Staples

Robert Staples, a sociology professor at the University of California in San Francisco, has published widely in the areas of race and family relations. In the following viewpoint, Staples argues that widespread discrimination is to blame for persistent poverty among African Americans. Although Staples recognizes the success of the black middle class, he takes issue with those who believe that black achievement is a sign of a fair and "color-blind" society. In Staples's opinion, racial discrimination limits opportunity for all blacks and ensures that many remain in poverty.

As you read, consider the following questions:

1. How does Staples define the "color-blind theory" of race relations in the United States?
2. According to the author, how do the incomes of black households compare with the incomes of white households?
3. What are the implications of PrimeTime Live's racial-discrimination experiment, in Staples's opinion?

From Robert Staples, "The Illusion of Racial Equality: The Black American Dilemma," in Lure and Loathing: Essays on Race, Identity, and the Ambivalence of Assimilation, edited by Gerald Early (New York: Penguin Books, 1993). Reprinted by permission.

N ever in the history of Homo sapiens has a society brought together so many cultural, religious, and racial groups in one country as the twentieth-century United States. Protestants, Catholics, Jews, Buddhists, Muslims, Italians, Africans, Chinese, Mexicans, Indians, all live together under the same government and operate in the same economy. This diversity is all the more striking when it is noted that none of these groups are at war with each other, that they coexist peaceably. This situation runs counter to the experiences of other countries in the world, where conflicts between ethnic and religious groups are epidemic. In 1986, more than five million people worldwide died as a result of ethnic and religious conflicts.

As a society dominated by people of European ancestry, the U.S.A. appears to have accommodated people of different national origins while European governments are besieged and in danger of being toppled by the small number of non-European immigrants allowed into their countries. Whereas most countries, in the latter part of the twentieth century, have permitted immigration on the basis of labor demand and personal wealth, American immigration policies have favored the family ties and refugee status of American citizens. Consequently, 85 percent of the legal immigration to the United States from 1973 to 1993 has involved citizens of Latin America, Asia, the Caribbean, and Africa. The white, non-Hispanic population in 1990 was recorded as 75 percent of the American population and, if current immigration and birthrate trends prevail, fewer than half of this country's citizens will be non-Hispanic whites in the year 2080. Further testament to the efficacy of the melting-pot theory is the high rate of intermarriage between these different groups. Most telling is the statistic that shows that Jews, a group that has faced persecution for most of its existence on this planet, have a minority of their members married within the same faith.

BLACK SUCCESS STORIES

It is within the Afro-American community that America's blend of free-wheeling capitalism and political democracy has produced the most startling success stories—or so it seems. Having come to the American continent, first as indentured servants, later as slaves, suffering from the most vicious form of segregation and discrimination in the postslavery era, they have risen to heights never envisioned for any group that occupied such low status. Jesse Jackson's slogan "From the outhouse to the White House" belies the struggle of this nation to keep its black population in a perpetually subjugated condition since their arrival.

Having used their labor, destroyed their culture and family life, the American version of apartheid and the caste system was erected after the official end of slavery. The white South created dual public institutions to degrade them, and states outside Dixie used informal rules to establish a ceiling on their aspirations and status. The black condition was best summed up in the saying: "No black shall ever rise above the lowest status of a white man."

Perforce, 1990s America has witnessed a dramatic turnaround of this country's determination to see and treat all black Americans as subhumans. This reversal did not come without a great deal of turmoil for a country whose self-definition is "the world's greatest democracy." It fought a bloody civil war over the issue of black slavery, perverted many of its institutions to protect racial inequality, endured mass demonstrations and protest against Jim Crow over a twenty-year period before officially eliminating the practice, and witnessed its major cities in flames during the 1960s as rebellions by blacks occurred throughout the nation. Because the civil rights movement and urban rebellions transpired during the expansionist and neo-colonial phase of capitalism, the pragmatic captains of industry and government decided that the caste line had to be abolished. Civil rights laws, recruitment of blacks into heretofore excluded positions, affirmative action regulations, loans, scholarships, social programs, set asides, and so on were gradually used to reduce the absolute caste line extant in 1940.

A LARGE BLACK MIDDLE CLASS

Those measures bore fruit in the 1990s when the world's largest black middle class was created. Overall, black Americans had a total income of $300 billion a year, a figure that equals the income of the twelfth-largest nation in the world. The median household income of black married couples, in 1990, was $33,893, giving them almost the highest standard of living in the world. Blacks also have a median educational level of 12.2 years, higher than most Europeans. More than a million blacks were enrolled in institutions of higher learning in 1991. More than other people of color, blacks appear to be integrated into the institutional life of American society. On the political level, they serve in the president's cabinet as his advisers, on the Supreme Court, as governors of states, as presidential candidates, as the head of the military, and as mayors of the nation's largest cities. In the major sports, amateur and professional, blacks dominate and earn millions of dollars in salaries and

commercial endorsements. Three of the five wealthiest enter-
tainers in America are black, the biggest box-office stars and
highest-rated TV shows have, in the past, been black, and the
largest sales of a record album are by a black performer. Not all
blacks in the entertainment industry are performers. In 1991,
two dozen theatrical films were directed by blacks, starring
black actors and actresses.

A RACIAL UTOPIA?

One might think that 1990s America is a racial utopia—or close
to it. Certainly a black sociologist from Harvard, Orlando Patterson, believed it to be true when he wrote in the New York Times
that "the sociological truths are that America, while still flawed
in its race relations and its stubborn refusal to institute a national, universal welfare system, is now the least racist white
majority society in the world; has a better record of legal protection of minorities than any other society, white or black; offers more opportunities to a greater number of black persons
than any other society, including those of Africa; and has gone
through a dramatic change in its attitude toward miscegenation
over the past 25 years." Professor Patterson is regarded as a
color-blind neo-conservative, which helps to explain his polly-
annaish view of race relations. Another view is held by an Afro-
American filmmaker, who has earned millions in the movie industry. Douglas McHenry is quoted as saying, "Today there is
probably more segregation and less tolerance than there was.
More than ever, there are two Americas."

Ironically, both men are essentially correct. The U.S., with a
white majority, has made more accommodations to its racial diversity than any other country largely composed of Europeans.
Even South American countries, with their pervasive pattern of
miscegenation, have reserved the most powerful and prestigious
positions for those most clearly identified as of European ancestry. The Patterson argument is most flawed when it depicts the
U.S. as "the least racist white majority society in the world."
However one defines racism in the 1990s, this country is more
racially segregated and its institutions more race driven than any
country outside South Africa. This fact, at least for the Euro-
American population, has been disguised by the emerging racial
ideology of the "color-blind theory." This theory has as its main
premise that after 365 years of slavery and legal segregation,
only 25 years of governmental laws and actions were necessary
to reverse the historical systematic and legalized segregation and
inequality in this country, and no further remedial effort is

needed. The net effect of the color-blind theory is to institution-alize and stabilize the status quo of race relations for the twenty-first century: white privilege and black deprivation. Most no-table among the proponents of the color-blind theory are the ideological descendants of the theories that slavery was neces-sary to make Christians out of African savages, that the South could operate separate but equal facilities and Jim Crow could not be abolished because it interfered with states' rights.

PAY DISPARITIES BY RACE AND GENDER

We cannot fall prey to the inane notion that discrimination is an evil of the past. It is today a very painful reality. . . . Representa-tion of women and people of color in the American workforce has improved, but is hardly sufficient. We still have a long way to go. When Affirmative Action was being enforced, gains were made, but during the Reagan-Bush years, many of the gains were lost. One need look no further than the well-documented dispar-ity in pay between white men, women, and people of color:

• In 1975, median income as a *percentage of white men's salaries* was 74% for African American men, 72% for Latino men, 58% for white women, 55% for African American women, and 49% for Latino women.

• At the height of the Reagan-Bush years in 1985, median income for African American men had dropped to 70%, for Latino men to 68%, rose for white women to 63%, and nominally increased to 57% for African American women and 52% for Latino women.

• In 1993, the figures reflect an increase for African American men to 74%, the rate for Latino men fell to 64%, 70% for white women, and 53% for African American women.

Jesse L. Jackson, press release, March 1, 1995.

The color-blind theory ignores the reality of 1990s America: that race determines everyone's life chances in this country. In any area where there is significant racial diversity, race impacts on where people live and go to school, whom they vote for, date, and marry, with whom they do business, whom they buy from or sell to, how much they pay, and so on. This does not sound like the racial utopia Martin Luther King dreamed of. In-deed, it may have been his worst nightmare. Yet there could be a worst nightmare for the prophet of racial equality. How would he have felt if he had watched his former lieutenants endorse the right-wing Ronald Reagan for president in 1980, or the or-ganization he founded, the Southern Christian Leadership Conference, remain neutral on the appointment of Clarence Thomas to the U.S. Supreme Court—a neutrality tantamount to the support provided by Strom Thurmond, Jesse Helms, and David Duke (former Grand Dragon of the Ku Klux Klan). The complexities of race in 1990s America are enough to confuse any outsider who has read the history of race relations in the U.S.

In part, to sort out the contradictions in American race relations, it is necessary to look at the other side of the black success story. Despite the largest black middle class in the world, the average black household income is only 56 percent of white household income. More than 32 percent of black households have incomes below the poverty line. The high income of black married-couple households is a function of multiple workers in those households. Moreover, poverty in the U.S. is increasingly synonymous with people of color. Only 8 percent of whites are considered poor, and they are disproportionately found among the elderly, women with children, and rural and farm families. Of all Western nations, the United States has the greatest inequality of wealth. According to an international study, poverty in the U.S. is more widespread and more severe: poor families here stay poor longer; and government programs of assistance are the least able to lift families with children out of poverty.

PERVASIVE POVERTY

Poverty also is more likely to be spread among the nonelderly households and to be widely distributed across all age and family groups. It is this class of poor people of color that make up a majority. In the more racially homogeneous countries of Europe, Australia, and New Zealand, government welfare programs and subsidies have eliminated the kind of massive poverty found among young households in this country. The tolerance of pervasive poverty, malnutrition, and homelessness can only be related to the perception that it is people of color who bear the brunt of American poverty and the reasons attributed to are their failure to get an education and work hard. When asked if the Federal Government should see to it that every person has a job and a good standard of living, 65 percent of blacks said it should, but only 24 percent of whites thought so. Euro-Americans were more inclined to give support to the idea of "individuals getting ahead on their own," versus government intervention. Surely the racial differences in attitude toward government assistance is linked to the fact that unemployment, for white male heads of households, is less than 6 percent, and as many as 46 percent of black males sixteen to sixty-two years of age are not in the labor force. Moreover, money is not the only measure of wealth in 1990s America. Noncash assets are easily convertible into cash. They include stocks, bonds, businesses, property, and so on, a total of $10 trillion. Given the concentration of wealth in the U.S., Euro-Americans will control 97 percent of those assets. Most blacks have only their homes and automobiles as assets. Because black homes tend to be located in black neighborhoods, their value is inherently less than those of similar homes in white neighborhoods.

Based on any variable that can be statistically measured, blacks have not achieved racial equality in any area of American life. And they are overrepresented on every negative variable except suicide, itself a mixed blessing since black suicide rates are highest among its young people in contrast to white suicide rates weighted toward its oldest members. And the direction of change in the U.S. has made some conditions worse than in the era before the civil rights movement. In 1950 the black unemployment rate was double that of whites: in 1990 it was triple. Housing and school segregation are worse outside the South in 1990 than in 1950. The inequality of wealth is greater in 1990 than in 1950, when most people earned money from wages. In the 1990s, people earn money, in larger numbers, from stocks, bonds, property, leveraged buyouts, etc. The percent of intact black families vis-à-vis white families was much higher in 1950 than in 1990, as was the lower number of black children born in wedlock. The times they are changing but things remain the same.

WIDESPREAD RACIAL DISCRIMINATION

For some reason this society documents but does not change many of its discriminatory practices. There are numerous studies, most of them conducted by Euro-Americans, showing the retention of racial discrimination in employment, housing, education, health care, and so on. One study found that 75 percent of black men seeking employment were discriminated against. In another investigation of housing discrimination, it was discovered that blacks face discrimination 56 percent of the time they seek to rent a house and 59 percent of the time they try to buy a home. Other studies reveal black patients in a hospital were more likely to be sent to inexperienced medical doctors and that car dealers were likely to charge Afro-Americans and women higher prices than white males. The number of studies showing racial discrimination in every facet of American life makes a mockery of the color-blind theory and Patterson's claim that this is the least-racist white majority society in the world.

Adding to the scholarly studies of racial discrimination are the TV shows, like 60 Minutes, which showed an employment agency using special codes to avoid sending black applicants to employers for jobs. On September 26, 1991, the show PrimeTime Live showed a nationwide audience what it's like to be black in 1990s America. They sent two twenty-eight-year-old men, Glen Brewer, black, and John Kuhnen, white, to shop in the same stores, attempt to rent the same apartment, and apply for the same job. Here are the results of their experiment in the city of St. Louis:

> At several stores, Mr. Kuhnen gets instant service: Mr. Brewer is ignored except at a record score, where a salesman keeps a close eye on him, without offering any assistance. When they go for a walk, separately on the same street, a police car passes Mr. Kuhnen but slows down to give Mr. Brewer a once-over. At a car dealership, Mr. Kuhnen is offered a lower price and better financing terms than Mr. Brewer. Inquiring about a job at a dry cleaner that has advertised for help, Mr. Kuhnen is told jobs are still available; Mr. Brewer is told, "The positions are taken." Following up a for-rent sign, Mr. Kuhnen is promptly offered an apartment, which he does not take; ten minutes later, Mr. Brewer is told it has been rented for hours.

That program gave Euro-Americans a visual lesson in the mundane indignities that many Afro-Americans experience day after day. Of course, only the most naïve white viewer should have been surprised at the results. Despite the color-blind theory, white claims of reverse racism and preferential treatment for blacks, there is no queue of whites claiming black heritage to qualify for the "benefits" of black membership. The color-blind theory is a smokescreen to mask the persistence of a racial hierarchy in American life.

"There is very little evidence . . . for the 'discrimination breeds poverty' hypothesis."

DISCRIMINATION DOES NOT CAUSE BLACK POVERTY

Byron M. Roth

In the following viewpoint, Byron M. Roth asserts that factors other than discrimination are responsible for low black income. Those who cite statistics on low black household income as proof of discrimination, he points out, often do not consider that many black families are headed by single women, while most white households consist of two-parent families. A single-parent family subsisting on one income is more likely to be poor than is a two-parent family living on multiple incomes, he maintains. In Roth's opinion, this difference in family structure—not discrimination—results in a higher poverty rate among African Americans. Roth is a professor of psychology at Dowling College in Oakdale, New York.

As you read, consider the following questions:

1. How does the author define the *ceteris paribus* assumption?
2. According to Roth, how did the composition of the black family change between 1960 and 1991?
3. What are some of the factors that can affect family income, in Roth's opinion?

From Byron M. Roth, *Prescription for Failure: Race Relations in the Age of Social Science* (New Brunswick, NJ: Transaction Publishers, 1994). Copyright 1994 by the Social Philosophy & Policy Center. Reprinted with permission.

Whether or not white Americans hold stereotyped and prejudiced views about blacks is a separate question from whether or not American whites discriminate against blacks. The question of discrimination is, in turn, separate from whether discrimination is effective. In general, the polling evidence supports the respected sociologist Rodney Stark when he says: "Again and again, researchers [have] found that the more education and income a person has, the less likely a person is to be prejudiced against other racial and ethnic groups." This suggests that those whites who express open hostility toward blacks, whatever their exact percentage, may not be in a position to hurt them, since they are likely to be concentrated among the least influential whites in society. If prejudiced whites do not hold positions of significant influence or power in American life, then they are not likely to be in a position to cause blacks economic or social harm. Of course, ignorant and prejudiced whites can cause blacks considerable emotional harm and can sometimes cause physical harm when they engage in violent criminal behavior. Nevertheless, it is difficult to see how this prejudiced minority can today do real and lasting economic damage to blacks.

AN UNREASONABLE ASSUMPTION

Some have argued that it is not so much that whites are prejudiced, but rather that American society has such a long history of racial separation and intolerance that institutions and practices that were put in place in support of separatism continue to exist, and make black success difficult. It is further argued that these institutions and practices are often so subtle as to be hard for either whites or blacks to detect. It is this "institutional" racism, some argue, rather than unconscious or symbolic racism on the part of individual whites, which holds blacks back.

The sheer magnitude of the income gap between blacks and whites is often cited to bolster this and other arguments for the existence of pervasive discrimination against blacks. The median income of black households in 1990 amounted to 58 percent of median white household income. This figure is almost unchanged from what it was in 1950, when black families had 54 percent of the median income of white families. The figure rose to 61 percent in 1970, but since then has dropped back to the 58 percent figure cited above, close to what it had been in 1950. The gap, therefore, between the incomes of black and white households is substantial and long-standing; it is a very large difference, and it is important to understand why it exists.

It is especially important to understand why, given all the effort to eliminate discrimination against blacks, the gap in family income has hardly changed at all in over forty years. To argue that this gap may be due to continuing discrimination is a hypothesis worth examining and testing. To assume, however, as do many, that the household incomes of blacks and whites would not differ at all were it not for the effects of discrimination, and to assume that other factors play no role, is, on its face, unreasonable. A scientific approach requires that we attempt to tease out all the factors and their relative importance, and not prematurely assign all the weight to this or that potential contributor.

OTHER FACTORS COULD CAUSE DISPARITIES

In order to make a legitimate scientific claim that discrimination causes economic hardship, one has first to satisfy what is known as the *ceteris paribus* assumption, the assumption that everything else is equal. For instance, if I claim that the income gap between male attorneys and female attorneys is due to discrimination, I must first control for other relevant factors that are known to contribute to the earning power of lawyers. In other words, I would have to show that a man and a woman who differed in no other way but their sex still differed in income. If I can do that, then I have made a case that discrimination is the cause. What this means in practice is that I must compare men and women who are matched for age, years of work in the profession, type of legal work, type of firm, hours worked, geographic location, quality of education, etc.

If I have done all that and a gap remains, then discrimination becomes a likely source of that gap. I have not, however, established proof for the discrimination hypothesis in any absolute sense, as I may have missed some important factors beside discrimination which could account for the difference. In any case, when one examines income differences between men and women or blacks and whites in this way, and one has controlled for fairly obvious factors, what at first seem very large income differences are usually narrowed and often disappear altogether. For instance, female lawyers earn less than male lawyers, but a large factor is age. In 1970, only 5 percent of law school graduates were women. By 1980, the figure rose to 30 percent, and by 1990, it was over 40 percent. The great majority of women practicing law today are relatively recent graduates, and very few have the seniority that commands high salaries. It will be interesting to compare the future salaries of men and women currently graduating law school to see if an income gap remains. If it does, will it be due to discrimination, or to the operation of other factors such as different personal expectations as to the meaning of work, family commitments, or some combination of factors?

RACE AND INCOME

Consider that while black men on average earn substantially less than white men, black women at all levels of education earn about the same as white women with comparable credentials. Remarkably, black women with college degrees earn more than white women with college degrees. This result directly contradicts the theory of discrimination which holds that black women are subject to the "double jeopardy" of both racism and sexism. Moreover, since black women are no less black than black men, their relative earnings parity with white women suggests the possibility that factors other than race might account for the black male earnings deficit.

Consider also that Mexicans, Puerto Ricans, and African Americans are a relatively young population. Mexican Americans and Puerto Ricans have a median age in the United States of under twenty-five, American Indians have a median age of twenty-six, African Americans have a median age of just over twenty-eight, while the American median is thirty-three, the median for many white ethnic groups is around thirty-five, and for American Jews is over forty. Since most people's earnings go up as their careers mature, age differences are clearly part of the reason for average race differences in earnings.

Dinesh D'Souza, *The End of Racism*, 1995.

Is the requirement of *ceteris paribus*, of holding all else equal, met by those who claim that black-white income disparities are due to discrimination? In most cases those who support the discrimination model make no attempt to see that "everything else is equal," and for that reason alone, their claim is suspect on scientific grounds. Thomas Sowell is one of the few who has actually performed the analysis which would determine the true effects of discrimination, and his results stand as a powerful, almost unassailable rebuttal to the civil rights vision. Without rehashing Sowell's extraordinarily thorough analysis, made in numerous books and articles throughout the 1980s, let me simply outline the main argument. The first and most important issue is that the figures above refer to *household* or *family* income. If one ethnic group tends to have more family members employed than another, then even if the individual members of each group are paid identical salaries, the group with more family members employed will have higher income. For that reason female-headed families almost always have smaller incomes than married-couple families.

Perusal of recent census data confirms Sowell's analysis. Census data for 1991 indicate that only 47.8 percent of all black families are married-couple families, compared to 82.8 percent of white families. Among families with children under eighteen the disparity is even greater. In 1991, only 37.4 percent of black families with children under eighteen were married-couple families, whereas among white families the figure was 77 percent. This is a powerful reason why there are so many poor black families today. In an age in which most middle-class families are supported by two wage-earners, any group with large numbers of families supported by one wage-earner will have much lower family income, even if those who do work earn exactly the same amount. In fact, with median married-couple family income fast approaching forty thousand dollars per year, it is almost impossible for most American families, unless they are headed by professionals, to attain middle-class status with only one income.

While there have always, in the twentieth century, been disparities in black and white family composition, recent trends have greatly exacerbated the problem. In 1960, for instance, 89.2 percent of white families (and 90 percent with children under eighteen) were married-couple families. Among black families in 1960, 77.7 percent were married-couple families and, of those with children under eighteen, 67 percent were. The upshot is that in the ensuing thirty years, while the incomes of individual black men and women were moving closer to parity with white incomes, black family income stagnated. No matter how you read the figures, most of the disparity in black-white family income results from the higher proportion of black families with only one wage-earner.

Single- Versus Two-Parent Families

Census figures indicate that in 1990, among all black families below the poverty line, 75 percent were headed by single women, while only 20 percent were married-couple families. Fifty-three percent of all black families with children under eighteen that were maintained by single women in 1990 were below the poverty line. By contrast, only 14.3 percent of black married-couple families with children were below the poverty line in that year.

There is a direct and important relationship between family income and family composition. In 1991, of those black families with children under eighteen, only 12 percent with incomes of $15,000 or less were two-parent families. By contrast, among those families with incomes over $25,000, 69 percent were two-parent families. Among black families with incomes over $40,000, fully 79 percent were two-parent families.

Between 1967 and 1990, the ratio of black to white median family income for all families hardly changed at all, and in fact declined slightly from the 59 percent figure in 1967. By way of contrast, the ratio of black to white median family income for married-couple families rose almost continuously during this period, from 68 percent in 1967 to 84 percent in 1990. These figures include older families formed before the important social changes of the fifties and sixties took place. Among married couples in the 15 to 24 year age range, the black-white income ratio was 94 percent in 1991. Among married couples in the 25 to 34 year age range, the ratio was 86 percent, and among those in the 35 to 44 year age range, the ratio was 92 percent. In other words, the median family income for married-couple black families formed in recent years approximates 90 percent of the income of white married-couple families.

The income figures for married couples are especially striking, because they include all sources of income, including investment income in the form of dividends, interest, and rent, as well as income from welfare payments, pensions, etc. A much larger percentage of whites have investment income than do blacks, not least of all because whites are much more likely, at present, to inherit wealth than are blacks. Investment income is very likely to be in addition to other income, while welfare rarely is. This factor in and of itself explains a large portion of the black-white income gap for married-couple families.

OTHER RELEVANT DATA

In addition, these figures do not take into account educational differences, unemployment differences, the employment status of spouses, geographic location, or a host of other factors affecting family income. When we factor in some of these variables, the income gap almost disappears. For instance, 55.8 percent of black families, but only 33 percent of white families, are located in the South, a region where incomes tend to be lower than in the rest of the country. Outside the South, median income for all black married-couple families was $39,462 and for white married-couple families it was $41,781, for a black-white ratio of

94.4 percent. In fact, among married-couple families outside the South where both husbands and wives worked, black families had median income of $46,657 and white families had median income of $46,094, for a black-white ratio of 101.2 percent.

This progress is illustrated by a recent analysis of the census data on Queens County of the City of New York by the *New York Times*. The *Times* reported that in 1989, the median income of black and white families in Queens was virtually identical. This data is especially impressive since it includes all families, single-parent as well as married-couple families. Median family income was $34,500 for blacks and $34,600 for whites. Queens has nearly two million residents, of whom about 20 percent are black. It is important to note that these figures are for family income, not merely wages, and therefore include interest, dividends, and other sorts of nonwage income. The black average in Queens was in excess of the state-wide average for all residents of $32,965.

There is very little evidence, therefore, for the "discrimination breeds poverty" hypothesis in the census figures. Black married-couple households that fit the predominant white pattern are beginning to approximate similar white families in their earning power, and may in fact have achieved parity if one factors in such things as investment income and the region in which people live. All of this does not mean that there is no discrimination in the workplace, but only that such discrimination as exists does not appear to hurt intact black families very much, especially when other factors are taken into account.

"Women as a group are as
economically disadvantaged in U.S.
society in the 1990s as they were
in 1960."

WOMEN FACE SIGNIFICANT
DISCRIMINATION

Sandra Lipsitz Bem

Many feminists agree that discrimination against women continues in American society despite antidiscrimination laws. In the
following viewpoint, Sandra Lipsitz Bem contends that widespread discrimination against women still exists primarily because the social world is organized from a male perspective. A
male-centered worldview, Bem argues, does not allow most
women to successfully balance work and childrearing. In Bem's
opinion, eliminating gender discrimination will require that
Americans restructure their societal institutions to meet the needs
of both women and men. Bem is a professor of psychology and
women's studies at Cornell University in Ithaca, New York.

As you read, consider the following questions:
1. What two arguments are typically used to explain "female
   inequality," according to Bem?
2. Why, in the author's opinion, have gender-neutral strategies
   to fight discrimination failed?
3. In what ways does a male-centered workplace limit women,
   according to Bem?

S ince the second half of the nineteenth century, the question of biological sex difference has been the focal point of virtually all American discussions of sexual inequality. It was at issue when the first American feminists were fighting to get women the most basic rights of citizenship and again when the second major wave of feminists swept onto the scene—and has been part of the discussion ever since. . . .

Implicit in this focus on sexual difference is the assumption that how the sexes *really* differ is a question of scientific and political urgency. I have argued, in contrast, that the question is scientifically misguided. In this viewpoint, I carry that argument a step further, suggesting that the focus on sexual difference is politically misguided as well. Specifically, I argue that if people in this androcentric [male-centered], gender-polarizing, and biologically essentialist culture are ever to understand why sexual equality would necessarily require a radical restructuring of social institutions, the cultural debate about sexual inequality must be reframed so that it addresses not male-female difference but how androcentric social institutions transform male-female difference into female disadvantage. . . .

PERSISTENT FEMALE INEQUALITY

In the current cultural debate, female inequality is typically attributed to one or the other of two causal factors, which need not be treated as mutually exclusive but usually are. Either women are being denied access to economic and political resources by policies and practices that intentionally discriminate against even those women whose situation is most similar to men's, in which case the consensus is that the government must step in to remedy the situation; or, alternatively, women's biological, psychological, and historical differences from men—especially their psychological conflict between career and family—lead them to make choices that are inconsistent with building the kind of career that would enable them to attain those economic and political resources, in which case there is no one to blame for female inequality and hence no consensus about any need for remediation.

Surprising as it may seem at first glance, recent economic studies have demonstrated that women as a group are as economically disadvantaged in U.S. society in the 1990s as they were in 1960, with only the subgroup of young, white, unmarried, and well-educated women showing any substantial economic progress and with everyone else so segregated into the lowest-paid occupations and part-time work that overall, women as a group still earn a mere 65 percent or so of what men earn. Although this persistent female inequality after thirty years of antidiscrimination law is frequently taken as evidence that discrimination against women is not nearly so important a cause of female inequality as female choice, I think this persistent female inequality is instead a testimony to the inadequacy of the understanding of how discrimination against women actually works.

THE GENDER-NEUTRAL STRATEGY

Ever since the Supreme Court ruled in *Muller v. Oregon* (1908) that protective legislation could be used to compensate women for their "disadvantage in the struggle for subsistence," two opposing strategies for ending female inequality have been at the center of the debate on gender policy. Gender neutrality, also known as gender blindness, mandates that no distinctions of any sort ever be made on the basis of sex; and special protection for women, also known as sensitivity to sexual difference, mandates that special provision be made in the workplace to compensate women for their biological and historical role as the caregivers for children.

The gender-neutral approach to sexual equality was popular during the 1960s and early 1970s, as indicated not only by the Supreme Court's willingness in *Reed v. Reed* to finally declare explicit discrimination against women to be unconstitutional but also by the willingness of almost all feminists of the day to enthusiastically support the passage of that most gender-blind of all feminist proposals, the equal rights amendment. The gender-neutral approach was so popular because it was consistent with three important facts that feminists were just then managing to bring to the attention of the general public: (1) discrimination on the basis of sex had long denied women the equal protection under the law that should have been guaranteed to all citizens by the Fourteenth Amendment to the U.S. Constitution; (2) protective legislation designed over the years to benefit women in the workplace had done more to hurt them economically than to help them; and (3) women are as inherently intelligent, responsible, and capable of supporting themselves, if given the opportunity to do so, as men—not inherently inferior, as legislators and judges traditionally represented them to be.

By the late 1970s and 1980s, however, champions of equal rights increasingly realized that gender neutrality so deemphasized the differences in the life situations of women and men that as a strategy, it was helping only those few women who were similarly situated to men while doing little, if anything, to help those many women who were locked into low-paying jobs by their gendered life situations as wives and mothers. Not only that, but when applied mindlessly and formulaically in divorce settlements, gender neutrality was actually harming differently situated women by falsely presupposing them to have as much earning potential—and hence as little need for alimony—as their husbands. Concentrating on this very large group of differently situated women highlighted the shortcomings of gender neutrality and thereby brought special protection back to center stage.

THE SPECIAL-PROTECTION STRATEGY

This time around, the advocates of special protection supported, not the kind of special limits for women that were at issue in *Muller v. Oregon*, but, instead, special benefits for women. Specifically, they proposed work-related policies designed to make it possible for women to be both highly paid workers and responsible primary parents, policies such as mandatory insurance coverage for pregnancy leave and a guaranteed return to one's job at the end of such a leave, paid days off for mothers of sick children, and even subsidized childcare. Although demands for these kinds of sex-specific arrangements in the workplace would have been beyond imagining in the difference-blind heyday of the equal rights amendment, they were not all that exceptional in an era when virtually all minority groups were vigorously asserting the values of pluralism and sensitivity to difference—including even physically disabled people, who were at last beginning to get the special access to the mainstream of American life that they need.

A great deal of support for these kinds of special benefits remains, as does a great deal of resistance to them. The support comes primarily from those feminists who see gender neutrality as having failed and, worse, as having required women to virtually become men to make it in the world of paid employment. The resistance comes from other feminists and from nonfeminists. . . .

A MALE-CENTERED REALITY

In 1984, the feminist legal scholar Catharine MacKinnon exposed the legal myth of gender neutrality as no other writer before her had done. Although she never actually used the term *androcentrism*, her basic argument was all but identical to the one in this viewpoint: although males and females differ from one another in many biological and historical characteristics, what is ultimately responsible for every aspect of female inequality, from the wage gap to the rape rate, is not male-female difference but a social world so organized from a male perspective that men's special needs are automatically taken care of while women's special needs are either treated as special cases or left unmet.

Consider, for example, the Supreme Court decisions on disability insurance coverage. Although the biological differences here are indisputable, the biological differences themselves were not the reason that pregnancy was excluded from insurance coverage while prostatectomies and circumcisions were included. The reason was a vision of gender neutrality so distorted by androcentrism that the male body was automatically taken as the standard, hence nothing seemed amiss when, in the name of equal protection, total and complete insurance coverage was granted for every one of a man's special needs but not for every one of a woman's.

© Clay Bennett. Reprinted with permission.

Consider, for another example, the critique of the legal definition of self-defense, which holds that a defendant can be found innocent of homicide only if he or she perceived imminent danger of great bodily harm or death and responded to that danger with only as much force as was necessary to defend against it. That definition always seemed to have nothing whatsoever to do with gender, but it no longer seems quite so gender neutral now that feminist legal scholars like Elizabeth Schneider and Phyllis Crocker have pointed out how much better it fits with a scenario involving two men in an isolated episode of sudden violence than with a scenario involving a woman being battered, first in relatively minor ways and then with escalating intensity over the years, by a man who is not only bigger and stronger than she is but from whom she cannot get police protection because he is her husband. The aha experience [recognition] here comes with the realization that if this woman and this situation had been anywhere near the center of the (male) policymakers' consciousness when they drafted the supposedly neutral definition of self-defense, they might not have placed so much emphasis on the defendant's being in imminent danger at the particular instant when the ultimate act of self-defense is finally made. . . .

THE WORK WORLD DOES NOT MEET WOMEN'S NEEDS

Of all the androcentric institutions that are typically considered gender neutral, perhaps none is more directly responsible for denying women their rightful share of economic and political resources in the United States than the structure of the work world. Many Americans may think that world of work is as gender neutral as it needs to be now that explicit discrimination against women has been made illegal, but it is, in fact, so thoroughly organized around a male worker with a wife at home to take care of the needs of the household—including childcare— that it transforms what is intrinsically just a male-female difference into a massive female disadvantage.

Imagine how differently the whole social world would be organized if there were no men around (reproduction would be handled somehow), and hence most of the workers in the workforce—including those at the highest levels of government and industry—were either pregnant or responsible for childcare during at least a certain portion of their adult lives. In this context, working would so obviously need to coordinate with birthing and parenting that institutions facilitating that coordination would be taken for granted. There would be paid pregnancy leave, paid days off to tend to sick children, paid childcare, and a match—rather than a mismatch—between the hours of the work day and the hours of the school day. There would probably also be a completely different definition of a prototypical work life, with the norm being not a continuous forty hours or more per week from adulthood to old age, but a transition from less than forty hours per week when the children were young to forty hours or more per week when the children were older.

The lesson of this alternative reality should be clear. Women's biological and historical role as mothers does not limit their access to economic and political resources. What limits access is an androcentric social world that provides but one institutionalized mechanism for coordinating work in the paid labor force with the responsibilities of being a parent: having a wife at home to take care of the children.

BALANCING WORK AND FAMILY

This institutional void affects different groups of women in different ways. Among mothers who work full-time when their children are young, for example, all but the wealthiest must endure the never-ending strain of struggling on their own to find decent and affordable childcare—which in the United States is neither decent nor affordable but all too often passes as such. They must also get up before dawn every weekday morning to take their youngest children to that childcare so that they can get themselves to work on time. All the while, they worry about whether their older children will get into any trouble during their several unsupervised hours before and after school and hope against hope that no school holidays will be declared that week and that none of the children comes down with a fever, because then they will have to leave a child at home alone all day or stay home from work. As if that were not enough to drive them to distraction, they also have to live every single day of their lives with the certain knowledge that—given the sorry state of childcare in the United States—their children are almost certainly not receiving the tender loving care or thoughtful and attentive supervision that they themselves would provide if only they could afford to stay at home while their children are young.

Given these difficulties, it is not surprising that women married to men with high earnings potential frequently make the decision to help maximize their husband's earnings—by, for example, supporting him through medical school before the children are born—so that, instead of having to coordinate paid work and family, they can stay home, at least until the children are in school, and, after that, limit the kinds of jobs they take to those that coordinate well with their children's school schedules. This seemingly rational arrangement may work fine financially for as long as the couple stays married, but if and when they get divorced, as couples often do in the United States, then every bit of the earnings potential that the couple has invested in during the years of their marriage will be embodied in the husband, and the wife will be left with no more ability to support herself on her own than she had when she entered the marriage.

The lives of two remaining groups of women in American society are also affected in dramatically different ways by the absence of institutional supports for coordinating work and family. The first group consists of all those highly career-oriented women who see no way to make it to the top of their fields except by remaining childless. This sacrifice is not ever required of men who make it to the top. In sharp contrast, the second group consists of all those single mothers on welfare, who are culturally stigmatized for their failure to have a male breadwinner in their home when, instead, they should be offered whatever institutional supports would enable them to carry out their dual responsibility as parent and provider.

This emphasis on the need for institutional supports to coordinate paid work and family may seem like just another example of special pleading on behalf of women. Not at all. It is a call for Americans to recognize that their social institutions do not reflect the needs and experiences of both women and men but instead reflect the needs and experiences of men. It is a call for Americans to reconstruct their social institutions to be so inclusive of both male and female experience that neither sex is automatically advantaged or disadvantaged by the social structure.

| "The more dangerous the [work] assignment, the more likely it is to be assigned to a man."

MEN FACE SIGNIFICANT DISCRIMINATION

Warren Farrell

Sex discrimination is often interpreted to mean discrimination against women. Men's rights activists, however, believe that men are also victimized in American society. In the following viewpoint, Warren Farrell points out that far more men than women work in hazardous professions. While men generally make more money than women, Farrell contends, men's jobs typically offer less flexibility, safety, and fulfillment than jobs traditionally filled by women. In the author's opinion, the expectation that men should be willing to risk their lives in these dangerous occupations is an unrecognized form of sex discrimination in the workplace. Farrell is the author of The Myth of Male Power, from which the following viewpoint is excerpted.

As you read, consider the following questions:

1. How does Farrell define the workplace's "glass cellar"?
2. According to the author, what dangers do garbage collectors face?
3. What kind of double standard do feminists apply when discussing hazardous jobs traditionally held by men, according to Farrell?

We frequently hear that women are segregated into low-paying, dead-end jobs in poor work environments such as factories. But when *The Jobs Related Almanac* ranked 250 jobs from best to worst based on a *combination* of salary, stress, work environment, outlook, security, and physical demands, they found that twenty-four of the twenty-five worst jobs were almost-all-male jobs. Some examples: truck driver, sheet-metal worker, roofer, boilermaker, lumberjack, carpenter, construction worker or foreman, construction machinery operator, football player, welder, millwright, ironworker. All of these "worst jobs" have one thing in common: 95 to 100 percent men.

Every day, almost as many men are killed at work as were killed during the average day in the Vietnam War. For men, there are, in essence, three male-only drafts: the draft of men to all the wars; the draft of Everyman to unpaid bodyguard; the draft of men to all the hazardous jobs—or "death professions." When men are not legally drafted, they feel psychologically drafted.

Just as women provide a womb to create the children, men often provide a financial womb to support the children. Many men are motivated to enter the death professions to provide this financial womb. The unspoken motto of the death professions is My Body, Not My Choice.

THE DEATH PROFESSIONS

- 94 percent of occupational deaths occur to men.
- The United States has a worker death rate three to four times higher than Japan's. If the U.S. had the same rate, we would save the lives of approximately 6,000 men and 400 women each year.
- The United States has only *one* job safety inspector for every *six* fish and game inspectors.
- Work safety is yet to become a course requirement for even one MBA program in the United States.
- Every workday hour, one construction worker in the United States loses his life.
- The more hazardous the job, the greater the percentage of men. Some examples are provided in Table I.

One reason the jobs men hold pay more is because they are more hazardous. The additional pay might be called the "Death Profession Bonus." And within a given death profession, the more dangerous the assignment, the more likely it is to be assigned to a man.

Both sexes contribute to the invisible barriers that both sexes experience. Just as the "glass ceiling" describes the invisible barrier that keeps women out of jobs with the most pay, the "glass cellar" describes the invisible barrier that keeps men in jobs with the most hazards.

TABLE I.	
MALE AND FEMALE PARTICIPATION IN DANGEROUS JOBS	
Hazardous Occupations	
Fire fighting	99% male
Logging	98% male
Trucking (heavy)	98% male
Construction	98% male
Coal Mining	97% male
Safe Occupations	
Secretary	99% female
Receptionist	97% female

Source: Warren Farrell, *The Myth of Male Power*, 1993.

Members of the glass cellar are all around us. But because they are our second-choice men, we make them invisible. (We hear women say, "I met this doctor . . . ," not "I met this garbage-man . . . .")

THE SECOND-CHOICE MAN

Let me tell you a little story.

I had just completed the research for this viewpoint and wanted to clear my mind. I thought an "errands morning" might do the trick. . . .

As I prepared to leave the house, I heard the roar of the garbage truck. Usually that just triggers an "Oh yeah, it's Monday." This time it also triggered my memory . . . that the garbageman was two and a half times more likely to be killed than a police officer. And that 70 percent of the collection crew for the City of San Diego (where I live) suffered job-related injuries in 1988 alone. Now, as I saw the garbageman pull up to my garbage, I connected the 70 percent figure to this man; to his disproportionate chances of back injuries, hernias, rectal cancer, cirrhosis of the liver, or just being hit by a passing automobile. I saw some things I hadn't seen before . . . first, just the lumbar support belt one of the men was wearing; then, eye contact; then, a name I had never bothered to ask. Ride with me for a moment on one of these men's trucks.

On Terry Hennesey's route (real person, true story) is a dental office. When he recently compacted the trash, several plastic bags of human blood burst and splattered into his face. Just a few weeks later, he found a World War II hand grenade with the pin still in it and about two dozen 9-millimeter, hollow-point bullets. Some months later he picked up a load of low-level radioactive waste. His colleagues tell stories of battery acid splattering on their clothes and faces; of the compacting process forcing chlorine to shoot out of a container, hitting a man in the back and setting him afire; of hot fireplace ashes being dumped in the trash and igniting the back of the truck; of a container of liquid cyanide. . . .

Why was I so unaware of these dangers? In part, because these men never speak up—instead they turn each other's misfortunes into humor, calling each other the "Cyanide Man," the "Radioactive Man," and so on. And in part, we are more conscious of the injuries of the football players, for example, because the absence of the football players has an impact on our egos: it makes "our team" lose. If our garbageman dies, he is replaced, like any part on the garbage truck.

MALE INVISIBILITY

I was more likely to think of it as sexism to call garbage collectors garbagemen than to understand that the real sexism is the pressure felt by uneducated, unskilled men to take more than 96 percent of the garbage collector jobs so they can get paid $9 to $15 an hour to support their families. Or that the real sexism was in hiding something dangerous in our garbage.

Once I saw the garbagemen in a different light, I registered how differently I looked at a garbageman as opposed to, say, a pregnant woman. When I see a pregnant woman, I automatically smile a smile that expresses appreciation for her joy, her adventure, her contribution. But I had never supported the garbageman with a smile that expressed appreciation for his contribution (although he supports what the pregnant woman creates and carries a different load). Nor had I felt empathy for his lack of joy . . . I never expected him to be joyful. For all practical purposes he had been invisible. As were so many men in the death professions. . . .

On my way to the Lucky supermarket in Encinitas, I picked up some cash from an ATM. At about the same time, an armed courier picked up cash from another ATM. He was the second armed courier to be fatally shot in the head that week. Every time I cash a check, an armed courier helps. Such couriers transport virtually every cent of cash that flows through the American economy. One of these couriers, a veteran of three combat tours in Vietnam and whose delivery area in south-central Los Angeles is gang-infested, says, "As soon as you open the door, you're 'meat on the table.'" So why do they do it? Well, as David Troy Nelson puts it, "I am a single parent with two preschool children." He is willing to be "meat on the table" so his two children might have meat on their table.

RISKING LIFE AND LIMB

Which brings me to the meat and vegetables. Sorting through chicken breasts, I used to be more aware of the crimes committed against chickens than those committed against the workers preparing the chicken. Of 2,000 workers at the Morrell meat packing plant, 800 had become disabled in one year. Some of these workers were chopping and carving at a rate of 1,000 movements per hour. With 40 percent per year being disabled, each worker's hands were essentially a time bomb. Almost 90 percent of the workers in the fifty-seven highest-risk jobs at Morrell were men. Dozens who had to undergo surgery requiring one to two months to heal were instead required to return to work immediately after the surgery.

As I picked out the best-looking vegetables, I took for granted that I would be washing off parathion and other poisons that allowed the best-looking vegetables to get that way. Now I found myself thinking of the men who spent their lives inhaling the parathion as it blew back into their faces from the planes and tractors from which they did their job of spraying.

I had always thought of farming as a reasonably safe profession in which men and women worked "side by side." I was wrong. With the exception of mining, the agricultural industry has the highest death rate of any industry. Young men are twenty-four times as likely to be killed in farm labor as are young women. They are also a lot more likely to suffer the amputation of an arm, leg, or finger. In reality, men and women do not work "side by side." Men work where there's greater potential for death; women, where there is greater potential for safety. As I picked up a microwave dinner, I felt thankful for the many men who prepared that dinner—who plowed, lifted, sprayed, and risked amputations so I could heat and eat a meal.

MALE FORMS OF NURTURING

As I exited from Lucky's down Encinitas Boulevard, I counted about thirty migrant workers in fewer than six blocks, each looking soulfully into the eyes of every passerby, each hoping to be picked to do a day's work in someone's fields. I saw a driver go by, look over the men, choose two, and leave the others behind. In the ten years I have lived in the town of Encinitas near San Diego, I have seen perhaps a thousand of these migrant workers waiting on these street corners. All of them have been men. Being rejected all day didn't mean returning to a warm home at night; it meant sleeping in the cold hills. In San Diego, these men are everywhere.

The field labor leaves the men permanently stooped over (after seven to ten years' work) and rips up their hands. The pesticides sprayed on the fields two or three times daily gradually soak into the men's skin, especially through open cuts on their hands. The poisons eventually deplete the men's brains or cause cancers. Those who make it back into the United States year after year to work in the fields thus face brain damage or early death (typically by age 40).

Most of these men are sending their wages back to their wives and children in Mexico, whom they see only once or twice a year before once again risking imprisonment by illegally crossing the U.S. border. This might be thought of as the migrant worker draft. Another all-male draft.

This "sacrifice-to-feed" is the male form of nurturance. In every class, men with families provide their own womb, the family's financial womb. They provide their bodies. But the psychology of disposability leaves them without placards reading My Body, My Choice. No movement calls these men oppressed for providing money for women from whom they are receiving neither cooking nor cleaning; for providing their wives with homes while they sleep on the ground. When a field worker is radicalized, he is taught to see the classism but remains blind to the sexism. Yet we call Mexican men patriarchs—as if the rules of their society served them at the *expense of women*.

DAILY WORK RISKS

As I stopped by a Vons supermarket for some grapefruit juice, I waited for a huge truck to back into a narrow delivery space. It was a familiar scene, but it was only as I had become aware of how truckers' scheduling demands sometimes led to their falling asleep at the wheel (making their death rate among the highest of any profession) that I registered the cup of coffee he was slugging down. In the process I saw more than a truck blocking my entrance into the parking lot, I saw a man in the truck. I visualized a trucker on his eighth cup of coffee at 4 A.M., stretching his limits so I can eat to my limit without paying to my limit.

I thought how I had been more likely to associate trucking with "teamsters" and the deaths caused by a truck accident rather than the deaths caused to the truckers. The difference in my feeling toward him turned a moment's wait into a moment's appreciation. I smiled at him with a warmth that must have been different because he returned the smile as if he felt the appreciation.

The impact was with me months later. As I saw Thelma and Louise and felt the audience's thunderous applause as they set a trucker's truck afire, I didn't miss what the audience felt, but I felt sad at what the audience was missing.

Before I returned home, I couldn't resist stopping by my fantasy house. It was being built on the bluffs over the ocean. As I watched the men putting nails through the lumber, I imagined the truckers navigating their semis through city traffic and the loggers navigating logs through half-frozen rivers (making logging one of the most dangerous of the death professions). I thought of logging lingo like "deadman" and "widowmaker" that referred to the various ways trees and branches could kill a man and make a widow. I realized my fantasy house would result not just from the risks taken by the construction workers but also by the truckers and loggers. . . .

A DOUBLE STANDARD

When mining, construction, and other death professions are discussed in feminist publications, they are portrayed as examples of the male power system, as "male-only clubs." However, when Ms. magazine profiled female miners, the emphasis was on how the woman was "forced" to take a job in the mines because it paid the best, and how taking such a job was the only way she could support her family.

Ms. could never acknowledge that the male-only clubs of hazardous occupations paid best because of their hazards and had been male-only exactly because men risked their lives for the extra pay to support their loved ones. They could not acknowledge that almost no woman worked in a mine to support a husband. Or that, if the woman they were profiling had a husband, he would have gone to the mines—not her. This double standard—of the death professions being a privilege when men did them and an oppression when women did them—has made two generations of men feel a bit unappreciated.

While twenty-four out of the twenty-five worst jobs are male jobs and many men also have low-pay jobs (busboy, doorman, dishwasher, gas station attendant, etc.), many of the lowest-paid jobs are predominantly occupied by women. Why the distinction between the "worst" and "low-paid" jobs? Because many of the low-paid jobs are low-paid because they are safer, have higher fulfillment, more flexible hours, and other desirable characteristics that make them more in demand and therefore lower in pay. When either sex chooses jobs with these desirable characteristics, they can expect low pay. Women are much more likely to choose jobs with seven of these eight characteristics—what might be called the "Female Occupations Formula."

Women now constitute 15–30 percent of a few of the high-pressure, highly skilled, and highly paid professions such as law and medicine. But occupations which employ more than 90 percent women almost always have in common at least seven of the following eight characteristics. The combination of all seven characteristics makes the job high in desirability—so high that an employer has more than enough qualified applicants and, therefore, does not need to pay as much.

- *Ability to Psychologically "Check Out"* at end of day (department-store clerk vs. lawyer)
- *Physical Safety* (receptionist vs. fire fighter)
- *Indoors* (secretary vs. garbage collector)
- *Low Risk* (file clerk vs. venture capitalist)
- *Desirable or Flexible Hours* (nurse vs. medical doctor)
- *No Demands to Move* out of town "or else"—to "move it or lose it" (corporate secretary vs. corporate executive)
- *High Fulfillment* relative to training (child-care professional vs. coal miner)
- *Contact with People* in a pleasant environment (restaurant hostess vs. long-distance trucker)

Note how this female occupations formula applies to the more than 90 percent female professions of receptionist, secretary, childcare professional, nurse, and department-store clerk or salesperson.

The "Exposure Professions"

After exposure to death, exposure to the elements is the most common hazard of male jobs. The hole in the ozone layer makes daily exposure to sun the equivalent of exposure to cancer, so the construction worker's newest hazard is invisible. And as for the road worker or garbage collector, well, not only does he take in ultraviolet rays through his skin but car fumes through his nose. All of which add the exposure professions to our list of death professions.

The more a worker's beat requires exposure to the sleet and the heat, the more likely is the worker to be a man: ditch digging, previously the work of chain gangs of prisoners, was protested as exploitive of prisoners. It is not protested as exploitive of men. The gas station attendant who pumps gas in the rain is most likely male (whereas the one collecting money indoors can be of either sex). Be it roofing or welding, if it is an exposure profession, it is a male profession.

The willingness to expose oneself to death at work belies a deeper male-female difference in attitude toward work. In a death profession, the feeling of not being entitled to protection is a metaphor. Harassment is called hazing, and hazing weeds out those who desire protection and selects for a team of protectors. Issues like hazing and harassment pale in comparison to the need to prevent death.

This doesn't mean that hazing and harassment are good for the individual. To the contrary: the very attitude that protects others is a disaster for protecting self—thus more New York City police commit suicide than are killed on duty.

Each man, whether in a coal mine near home or in a trench "over there," *expects* his body to be used. Male prostitution is a given; freedom from it, a luxury. Which is why the unspoken motto of the death professions is My Body, Not My Choice.

In brief, then, it is a myth that women are segregated into the worst jobs. Jobs that require few skills and few hazards pay less and jobs that have high fulfillment pay less—to *either* sex. The worst jobs are almost all "male jobs," which men take more because they have, on average, more mouths to feed.

"Politicians and media people talk about 'illegal aliens' to dehumanize and demonize undocumented immigrants, who are for the most part people of color."

ANTI-IMMIGRATION MEASURES ARE DISCRIMINATORY

Leslie Marmon Silko

In the following viewpoint, Leslie Marmon Silko contends that the U.S. Border Patrol mistreats people of color, immigrants, and white people whose appearance or behavior suggests that they may be aiding illegal immigrants. The fact that the Border Patrol is allowed to detain the occupants of any vehicle violates U.S. residents' rights to travel freely, she asserts. In Silko's opinion, many anti-immigration measures—including legal detainment, intimidation, and extensive vehicle and body searches—are discriminatory and unwarranted. Silko is the author of the novels *Ceremony* and *Almanac of the Dead*.

As you read, consider the following questions:

1. What comparison does Silko make between the United States in the 1990s and Argentina in the 1970s?
2. How does Silko describe her own nighttime experience with the Border Patrol in New Mexico?
3. In the author's opinion, why are borders ineffective?

From Leslie Marmon Silko, "The Border Patrol State," *Nation*, October 17, 1994. Reprinted with permission from the *Nation* magazine, ©1994.

I used to travel the highways of New Mexico and Arizona with a wonderful sensation of absolute freedom as I cruised down the open road and across the vast desert plateaus. On the Laguna Pueblo reservation, where I was raised, the people were patriotic despite the way the U.S. government had treated Native Americans. As proud citizens, we grew up believing the freedom to travel was our inalienable right, a right that some Native Americans had been denied in the early twentieth century. Our cousin, old Bill Pratt, used to ride his horse 300 miles overland from Laguna, New Mexico, to Prescott, Arizona, every summer to work as a fire lookout.

In school in the 1950s, we were taught that our right to travel from state to state without special papers or threat of detainment was a right that citizens under communist and totalitarian governments did not possess. That wide open highway told us we were U.S. citizens; we were free. . . .

AN ENCOUNTER WITH THE BORDER PATROL

Not so long ago, my companion Gus and I were driving south from Albuquerque, returning to Tucson after a book promotion for the paperback edition of my novel *Almanac of the Dead*. I had settled back and gone to sleep while Gus drove, but I was awakened when I felt the car slowing to a stop. It was nearly midnight on New Mexico State Road 26, a dark, lonely stretch of two-lane highway between Hatch and Deming. When I sat up, I saw the headlights and emergency flashers of six vehicles—Border Patrol cars and a van were blocking both lanes of the highway. Gus stopped the car and rolled down the window to ask what was wrong. But the closest Border Patrolman and his companion did not reply; instead, the first agent ordered us to "step out of the car." Gus asked why, but his question seemed to set them off. Two more Border Patrol agents immediately approached our car, and one of them snapped, "Are you looking for trouble?" as if he would relish it.

I will never forget that night beside the highway. There was an awful feeling of menace and violence straining to break loose. It was clear that the uniformed men would be only too happy to drag us out of the car if we did not speedily comply with their request (asking a question is tantamount to resistance, it seems). So we stepped out of the car and they motioned for us to stand on the shoulder of the road. The night was very dark, and no other traffic had come down the road since we had been stopped. All I could think about was a book I had read—*Nunca Más*—the official report of a human rights commission that investigated and certified more than 12,000 "disappearances" during Argentina's "dirty war" in the late 1970s.

The weird anger of these Border Patrolmen made me think about descriptions in the report of Argentine police and military officers who became addicted to interrogation, torture and the murder that followed. When the military and police ran out of political suspects to torture and kill, they resorted to the random abduction of citizens off the streets. I thought how easy it would be for the Border Patrol to shoot us and leave our bodies and car beside the highway, like so many bodies found in these parts and ascribed to "drug runners."

A CONTRABAND SEARCH

Two other Border Patrolmen stood by the white van. The one who had asked if we were looking for trouble ordered his partner to "get the dog," and from the back of the van another patrolman brought a small female German shepherd on a leash. The dog apparently did not heel well enough to suit him, and the handler jerked the leash. They opened the doors of our car and pulled the dog's head into it, but I saw immediately from the expression in her eyes that the dog hated them, and that she would not serve them. When she showed no interest in the inside of our car, they brought her around back to the trunk, near where we were standing. They half-dragged her up into the trunk, but still she did not indicate any stowed-away human beings or illegal drugs.

Their mood got uglier; the officers seemed outraged that the dog could not find any contraband, and they dragged her over to us and commanded her to sniff our legs and feet. To my relief, the strange violence the Border Patrol agents had focused on us now seemed shifted to the dog. I no longer felt so strongly that we would be murdered. We exchanged looks—the dog and I. She was afraid of what they might do, just as I was. The dog's handler jerked the leash sharply as she sniffed us, as if to make her perform better, but the dog refused to accuse us: She had an innate dignity that did not permit her to serve the murderous impulses of those men. I can't forget the expression in the dog's eyes; it was as if she were embarrassed to be associated with them. I had a small amount of medicinal marijuana in my purse that night, but she refused to expose me. I am not partial to dogs, but I will always remember the small German shepherd that night.

Unfortunately, what happened to me is an everyday occurrence here now. Since the 1980s, on top of greatly expanding border checkpoints, the Immigration and Naturalization Service and the Border Patrol have implemented policies that interfere with the rights of U.S. citizens to travel freely within our borders. I.N.S. agents now patrol all interstate highways and roads that lead to or from the U.S.-Mexico border in Texas, New Mexico, Arizona and California. Now, when you drive east from Tucson on Interstate 10 toward El Paso, you encounter an I.N.S. check station outside Las Cruces, New Mexico. When you drive north from Las Cruces up Interstate 25, two miles north of the town of Truth or Consequences, the highway is blocked with orange emergency barriers, and all traffic is diverted into a two-lane Border Patrol checkpoint—ninety-five miles north of the U.S.-Mexico border.

EVERY RIGHT TO BE HERE

As long as we have a rich country in the North and severe poverty and repression in Latin America and Asia, people are going to flee looking for work to feed themselves and their families, just as millions of Germans, Greeks, Italians, Jews, Irish, Poles, and Russians did before them. Among the issues not reported by the media and the racially motivated right wing groups is that the largest populations of undocumented persons in the U.S. today are Canadians, Irish, Poles, and Russians, not Mexicans or Haitians. And these persons are seldom pursued by the INS. And recall that California, Texas and most of the Southwest was once part of Mexico. Latinos and indigenous people have every bit as much right to live and work in peace in this land as do Anglos.

Pamphlet, Democratic Socialists of America, 1995.

I was detained once at Truth or Consequences, despite my and my companion's Arizona driver's licenses. Two men, both Chicanos, were detained at the same time, despite the fact that they too presented ID and spoke English without the thick Texas accents of the Border Patrol agents. While we were stopped, we watched as other vehicles—whose occupants were white—were waved through the checkpoint. White people traveling with brown people, however, can expect to be stopped on suspicion they work with the sanctuary movement, which shelters refugees. White people who appear to be clergy, those who wear ethnic clothing or jewelry and women with very long hair or very short hair (they could be nuns) are also frequently detained; white men with beards or men with long hair are likely to be detained, too, because Border Patrol agents have "profiles" of "those sorts" of white people who may help political refugees. (Most of the political refugees from Guatemala and El Salvador are Native American or mestizo [of mixed Indian and European heritage] because the indigenous people of the Americas have continued to resist efforts by invaders to displace them from their ancestral lands.) Alleged increases in illegal immigration by people of Asian ancestry means that the Border Patrol now routinely detains anyone who appears to be Asian or part Asian, as well.

Once your car is diverted from the Interstate Highway into the checkpoint area, you are under the control of the Border Patrol, which in practical terms exercises a power that no highway patrol or city patrolman possesses: They are willing to detain anyone, for no apparent reason. Other law-enforcement officers need a shred of probable cause in order to detain someone. On the books, so does the Border Patrol; but on the road, it's another matter. They'll order you to stop your car and step out; then they'll ask you to open the trunk. If you ask why or request a search warrant, you'll be told that they'll have to have a dog sniff the car before they can request a search warrant, and the dog might not get there for two or three hours. The search warrant might require an hour or two past that. They make it clear that if you force them to obtain a search warrant for the car, they will make you submit to a strip search as well.

TRAVELERS FEEL VIOLATED

Traveling in the open, though, the sense of violation can be even worse. Never mind high-profile cases like that of former Border Patrol agent Michael Elmer, acquitted of murder by claiming self-defense, despite admitting that as an officer he shot an "illegal" immigrant in the back and then hid the body, which remained undiscovered until another Border Patrolman reported the event. (In September 1994, Elmer was convicted of reckless endangerment in a separate incident, for shooting at least ten rounds from his M-16 too close to a group of immigrants as they were crossing illegally into Nogales in March 1992.) Or that in El Paso, a high school football coach driving a vanload of his players in full uniform was pulled over on the freeway and a Border Patrol agent put a cocked revolver to his head. (The football coach was Mexican-American, as were most of the players in his van; the incident eventually caused a federal judge to issue a restraining order against the Border Patrol.) We've a mountain of personal experiences like that which never make the newspapers. A history professor at U.C.L.A. told me she had been traveling by train from Los Angeles to Albuquerque twice a month doing research. On each of her trips, she had noticed that the Border Patrol agents were at the station in Albuquerque scrutinizing the passengers. Since she is six feet tall and of Irish and German ancestry, she was not particularly concerned. Then one day when she stepped off the train in Albuquerque, two Border Patrolmen accosted her, wanting to know what she was doing, and why she was traveling between Los Angeles and Albuquerque twice a month. She presented identification and an explanation deemed "suitable" by the agents, and was allowed to go about her business.

Just the other day, a friend told me about his 73-year-old father, who is half Chinese and had set out alone by car from Tucson to Albuquerque the week before. His father had become confused by road construction and missed a turnoff from Interstate 10 to Interstate 25; when he turned around and circled back, he missed the turnoff a second time. But when he looped back for yet another try, Border Patrol agents stopped him and forced him to open his trunk. After they satisfied themselves that he was not smuggling Chinese immigrants, they sent him on his way. He was so rattled by the event that he had to be driven home by his daughter.

This is the police state that has developed in the southwestern United States since the 1980s. No person, no citizen, is free to travel without the scrutiny of the Border Patrol. In the city of South Tucson, where 80 percent of the respondents were Chicano or Mexicano, a joint research project by the University of Wisconsin and the University of Arizona recently concluded that one out of every five people there had been detained, mistreated verbally or nonverbally, or questioned by I.N.S. agents in the past two years.

U.S. POLICY IS DEHUMANIZING

Manifest Destiny may lack its old grandeur of theft and blood—"lock the door" is what it means now, with racism a trump card to be played again and again, shamelessly, by both major political parties. "Immigration," like "street crime" and "welfare fraud," is a political euphemism that refers to people of color. Politicians and media people talk about "illegal aliens" to dehumanize and demonize undocumented immigrants, who are for the most part people of color. Even in the days of Spanish and Mexican rule, no attempts were made to interfere with the flow of people and goods from south to north and north to south. It is the U.S. government that has continually attempted to sever contact between the tribal people north of the border and those to the south. [The Treaty of Guadalupe Hidalgo, signed in 1848, recognizes the right of the Tohano O'Odom (Papago) people to move freely across the U.S.-Mexico border without documents. A treaty with Canada guarantees similar rights to those of the Iroquois nation in traversing the U.S.-Canada border.]

Now that the "Iron Curtain" is gone, it is ironic that the U.S. government and its Border Patrol are constructing a steel wall ten feet high to span sections of the border with Mexico. While politicians and multinational corporations extol the virtues of NAFTA [the North American Free Trade Agreement] and "free trade" (in goods, not flesh), the ominous curtain is already up in a six-mile section at the border crossing at Mexicali; two miles are being erected but are not yet finished at Naco; and at Nogales, sixty miles south of Tucson, the steel wall has been all rubber-stamped and awaits construction. Like the pathetic multimillion-dollar "antidrug" border surveillance balloons that were continually deflated by high winds and made only a couple of meager interceptions before they blew away, the fence along the border is a theatrical prop, a bit of pork for contractors. Border entrepreneurs have already used blowtorches to cut passageways through the fence to collect "tolls," and are doing a brisk business. Back in Washington, the I.N.S. announces a $300 million computer contract to modernize its record-keeping and Congress passes a crime bill that shunts $255 million to the I.N.S. for 1995, $181 million earmarked for border control, which is to include 700 new partners for the men who stopped Gus and me in our travels, and the history professor, and my friend's father, and as many as they could from South Tucson.

THE GREAT HUMAN MIGRATION

It is no use; borders haven't worked, and they won't work, not now, as the indigenous people of the Americas reassert their kinship and solidarity with one another. A mass migration is already under way; its roots are not simply economic. The Uto-Aztecan languages are spoken as far north as Taos Pueblo near the Colorado border, all the way south to Mexico City. Before the arrival of the Europeans, the indigenous communities throughout this region not only conducted commerce, the people shared cosmologies, and oral narratives about the Maize Mother, the Twin Brothers and their Grandmother, Spider Woman, as well as Quetzalcoatl the benevolent snake. The great human migration within the Americas cannot be stopped; human beings are natural forces of the Earth, just as rivers and winds are natural forces.

Deep down the issue is simple: The so-called "Indian Wars"

from the days of Sitting Bull and Red Cloud have never really ended in the Americas. The Indian people of southern Mexico, of Guatemala and those left in El Salvador, too, are still fighting for their lives and for their land against the "cavalry" patrols sent out by the governments of those lands. The Americas are Indian country, and the "Indian problem" is not about to go away.

One evening at sundown, we were stopped in traffic at a railroad crossing in downtown Tucson while a freight train passed us, slowly gaining speed as it headed north to Phoenix. In the twilight I saw the most amazing sight: Dozens of human beings, mostly young men, were riding the train; everywhere, on flat cars, inside open boxcars, perched on top of boxcars, hanging off ladders on tank cars and between boxcars. I couldn't count fast enough, but I saw fifty or sixty people headed north. They were dark young men, Indian and mestizo; they were smiling and a few of them waved at us in our cars. I was reminded of the ancient story of Aztlán, told by the Aztecs but known in other Uto-Aztecan communities as well. Aztlán is the beautiful land to the north, the origin place of the Aztec people. I don't remember how or why the people left Aztlán to journey farther south, but the old story says that one day, they will return.

"Unrestrained immigration is producing 'a leveling down of American society.'"

ANTI-IMMIGRATION MEASURES ARE NECESSARY

William Norman Grigg

Uncontrolled immigration threatens America's unity and freedom, William Norman Grigg asserts in the following viewpoint. He maintains that changes to U.S. immigration policies have led to an increase in both legal and illegal immigration from non-Western and third world countries. According to Grigg, many of these newer immigrants come to the United States to take advantage of welfare services and racial-preference benefits at a high cost to taxpayers. Furthermore, Grigg contends that this large wave of immigration has fueled ethnic separatism and dangerously subversive politics. Stronger borders and stricter anti-immigration measures are therefore needed, he argues, to protect America's institutions. Grigg is a senior editor for the *New American*, a biweekly conservative journal.

As you read, consider the following questions:

1. According to the author, how is the "dogma of 'diversity'" affecting America?
2. What does Grigg say was the purpose of the Immigration Reform Act of 1965?
3. What are the Mexican government's intentions in regards to American Hispanics, in Grigg's opinion?

From William Norman Grigg, "Revolution in America," *New American*, February 19, 1996. Reprinted by permission.

"I am not an American. There is nothing about me that is American. I don't want to be an American, and I have just as much right to be here as any of you." Thus spoke one individual identified as a "Latino activist" during a session of the "National Conversation on American Pluralism and Identity," a $4 million project funded by the National Endowment for the Humanities (NEH). NEH Director Sheldon Hackney reacted to this hateful outburst by cooing, "What an American thing to say—squarely in the great tradition of American dissent. He was affirming his American identity even as he was denying it."

From Hackney's perspective, there are none so American as those who hate this country. Unfortunately, a similar concept of the American identity governs our present immigration policies. Guided by the dogma of "diversity," the political establishment has rejected the traditional goal of assimilation, choosing instead to create a Babel of querulous ethnic interest groups squabbling over government largesse and united only through the political power of the state. . . .

AMERICA'S IMMIGRATION POLICY

To understand how the present state of affairs came about, and how it may be remedied, it is necessary to review America's traditional immigration policy.

Throughout its history, America's philosophy of God-given individual rights and institutions of ordered liberty have attracted immigrants from around the globe. However, from our nation's founding until 1965, American policymakers understood that immigration is a *privilege*, not an unalienable *right*— and that this nation, like every sovereign nation, may properly regulate immigration in its own interests. Dr. Charles Rice, a professor of law at Notre Dame University, observes that "with respect to nonresident aliens, their admission to the country is subject to the virtually plenary power of Congress."

This is not to say that Congress may regard aliens as "nonpersons"; rather, it is to acknowledge that such people do not possess the procedural rights and immunities which are enjoyed by American citizens, and that their admission to this country is contingent on their qualifications for productive citizenship. In his report on immigration to the First Congress, James Madison urged that America "welcome every person of good fame [who] really means to incorporate himself into our society, but repel all who will not be a real addition to the wealth and strength of the United States."

America's political system, economy, and cultural institutions are derivative of Anglo-European traditions; accordingly, American immigration policies traditionally favored English-speaking immigrants from Europe who could be readily assimilated into our society. Additionally, during the last "great wave" of immigration (which lasted roughly from 1890 to 1920), the absence of a welfare state made assimilation a necessity. Peter Brimelow estimates, "At the turn of the century, 40 percent of all immigrants went home, basically because they failed in the work force." However, millions of immigrants succeeded in America's economy and embraced American ideals.

Even before the advent of the welfare state, however, social pressures attendant to the "great wave" created support for tighter immigration controls. The Immigration Acts of 1921 and 1924 were intended to preserve a stable *status quo* by imposing a national origins quota system. The McCarran-Walter Act of 1952 retained the basic structure of the 1924 measure, while adding important provisions intended to prevent the admission of known subversives to America's shores.

INVERTED PRIORITIES

However, the passage of the Immigration Reform Act of 1965 infused an entirely different set of values and priorities into our basic immigration law. Simply put, the effect of the 1965 immigration law was to define American immigration policies by our nation's supposed obligation to the rest of the world, rather than by a sound definition of our own national interest. As Senator Robert F. Kennedy (D-NY) stated during the debate over the 1965 law, the measure assumed that "the relevant community is not merely the nation, but all men of goodwill."

One expressed intention of the measure was proportionately to increase immigration from non-Western nations; this was accomplished by abolishing the national origins quota system. Furthermore, although the formal immigration quota was raised only slightly, the measure allowed for theoretically unlimited "non-quota" immigration for refugees, asylum seekers, and relatives of naturalized citizens for purposes of "family reunification" (also known as "chain immigration").

Many critics of the 1965 measure predicted that its passage would result in a torrential surge of unassimilable immigrants, resulting in profound social dislocations. Senator Edward Kennedy (D-MA), who served as Senate floor manager for S. 500 (the Senate version of the measure), parried such objections by offering these assurances of what the bill supposedly would not do:

First, our cities will not be flooded with a million immigrants annually. Under the proposed bill, the present level of immigration remains substantially the same. . . . Secondly, the ethnic mix of this country will not be upset. . . . Contrary to the charges in some quarters, S. 500 will not inundate America with immigrants from any one country or area, or the most populated and economically deprived nations of Africa and Asia. . . . In the final analysis, the ethnic pattern of immigration under the proposed measure is not expected to change as sharply as the critics seem to think.

THE POST-1965 INFLUX

. . . As Peter Brimelow observes, "Every one of Senator Kennedy's assurances has proven false. Immigration levels did surge upward. They are now running at around a million a year, not counting illegals. Immigrants do come predominantly from one area—some 85 percent of the 16.7 million legal immigrants arriving in the United States between 1968 and 1993 came from the Third World: 47 percent from Latin America and the Caribbean; 34 percent from Asia. . . . Also, immigrants did come disproportionately from one country—20 percent from Mexico." Nearly two million immigrants arrived in 1991 alone, and the 1990s rate is at least one million immigrants per year—a figure which exceeds the number of immigrants admitted by the rest of the industrial nations combined.

Taken by itself, such an influx would have enormously unsettling social, cultural, and economic effects. However, when coupled with the welfare state and racial spoils system which presently exist in this country, the post-1965 immigrant wave has proven to be uniquely disruptive. Liberal commentator Michael Lind, who does not reject the welfare/affirmative action state in principle, points out, "As a proportion of the U.S. population, the groups eligible for racial preference benefits are rapidly growing, thanks to mass immigration from Latin America and Asia."

While earlier European immigrants were under the necessity of assimilating quickly, Lind observes that "today's Hispanic and Asian immigrants are tempted by a variety of rewards for retaining their distinctive racial identities, even their different languages":

> The moment a Mexican or Chinese immigrant becomes a naturalized citizen of the United States, he can qualify for special consideration in admission to colleges and universities, at the expense of better-qualified white Americans; expect and receive

special treatment in employment; apply for minority business subsidies denied to his neighbors; and even demand to have congressional district lines redrawn to maximize the likelihood of electing someone of his race or ethnic group. . . .

These perks and privileges are sources of ethnic tensions and considerable public expense. In a 1993 study, economist Donald Huddle of Rice University documented that "immigrants cost the American taxpayer more than $42.5 billion in 1992 alone" for services such as subsidized education, Medicaid, health and welfare services, bilingual education, and Aid to Families with Dependent Children. Should the present immigration policies remain in place, Huddle asserted, the cost of welfare subsidies to immigrants between 1993 to 2002 would average "$67 billion per year in 1992 dollars, a net total of $668.5 billion after taxes over the decade."

BORDER BREAKDOWN

Beyond the problems created by legal immigration are those precipitated by the breakdown of the "thin green line"—the Immigration and Naturalization Service (INS) and its Border Patrol, which are supposed to maintain the integrity of our borders against illegal immigration. "Illegal immigrants come from all over the world," reported the November 26, 1993, *Los Angeles Times*. "They come in rickety boats. They arrive on jetliners with valid business, student or tourist visas and then ignore the expiration date and stay here illegally. They enter on forged documents or fraudulent employment visas. They contract sham marriages to U.S. citizens." Most illegal immigrants enter the U.S. across our 2,000-mile border with Mexico.

How many illegals enter the U.S. every year? "We don't know—that's the bottom line," says INS spokesman Robert Stiev. It's almost as if we were asked, 'How many fish didn't you catch?'" An INS study in 1992 estimated that 3.4 million illegal immigrants had taken up residence in the United States, with another 300,000 arriving every year. To stem this tide, the Border Patrol has been assigned fewer than 5,000 agents and allocated a budget of $584 million—a pitiful pool of resources when compared, for example, to the 32,000 U.S. servicemen and $2 billion to $3 billion which has been set aside to patrol the artificial borders of the "nation" of Bosnia. . . .

ETHNIC SEPARATISM

Immigration reform advocate Richard Estrada observes that unrestrained immigration is producing "a leveling down of American society, which in turn could be accompanied by an intensification of tribalist politics, ethnic and linguistic separatism, and finally the further debasement of the coin of individual initiative, freedom, and liberty." The fissiparous [divisive] tendencies which concern Estrada are most pronounced along America's border with Mexico.

ETHNIC ENCLAVES

Lacking any pressures to assimilate, utterly ignorant of the beliefs of our Founding Fathers, and seduced by contemporary leftist propaganda that inculcates the newly arrived with stories of oppression by a white-dominated society, immigrants now tend to form ethnic enclaves and are enticed by radical organizations that promise to fight for their "rights." Unfortunately, these so-called rights tend to be seen in terms of specific "group rights," a trend that has balkanized many inner city areas and promises eventually to do the same to the whole country. As immigrants become voting citizens they tend to become ethnic-bloc voters, supporting candidates who promise their particular group the "best deal" in tax-subsidized goodies. In short, an immigration policy that, because it was limited and moderate, was once a source of strength for the country has now been turned against us and is a source of grave concern for our future.

James Thornton, *New American*, February 19, 1996.

According to Henry Cisneros, the Clinton Administration's Secretary of Health and Human Services, the effective breakdown of the border between the U.S. and Mexico is resulting in "the Hispanization of America. . . . It is already happening and it is inescapable." Less sanguine observers would refer to this development as an *invasion*. While some might shrink from using the term, "invasion" was the word used to describe the Mexican exodus to the U.S. in a 1982 article published in *Excelsior*, Mexico's equivalent of the *New York Times*. In "The Great Invasion: Mexico Recovers Its Own," *Excelsior* columnist Carlos Loret de Mola examined the cultural and political implications of uncontrolled Mexican immigration to the U.S.:

A peaceful mass of people . . . carries out slowly and patiently an unstoppable invasion, the most important in human history. You cannot give me a similar example of such a large migratory wave by an ant-like multitude, stubborn, unarmed, and carried on in the face of the most powerful and best-armed nation on earth. . . . [Neither] barbed-wire fences, nor aggressive border guards, nor campaigns, nor laws, nor police raids against the undocumented, have stopped this movement of the masses that is unprecedented in any part of the world.

THE AZTLAN LEGEND

According to Loret, the migrant invasion "seems to be slowly returning [the southwestern United States] to the jurisdiction of Mexico without the firing of a single shot, nor requiring the least diplomatic action, by means of a steady, spontaneous, and uninterrupted occupation." The effects of Mexico's immigration invasion were even then visible in Los Angeles, which Loret cheekily referred to as "the second largest Mexican city in the world."

Loret's essay invoked the irredentist fantasy that California, Arizona, New Mexico, Colorado, and Texas—the states created in the territory obtained from Mexico through the Treaty of Guadalupe Hidalgo in 1848—compose "Aztlan," the mythical homeland of the Aztec Indians, and that those states must be wrested from the United States in order to create a new Chicano homeland. More than a quarter of a century ago, political analyst Patty Newman warned that "the basic concept of El Plan de Aztlan is endorsed by most of the major Mexican-American organizations on campus and off, liberal and supposedly conservative." Believers in the Aztlan legend insist upon the indivisibility of "la Raza" (the Mexican race) and the need to abolish the border between the U.S. and Mexico; one of their preferred slogans is, "We didn't cross the border—the border crossed us.". . .

MEXICAN MEDDLING

Although the literature of radical Chicano activists is replete with criticism of the Mexican government, . . . the Mexican establishment is actually pursuing the same ends which define the Chicano movement in the U.S.: The effective eradication of the border and the political consolidation of Mexicans within this country. The December 10, 1995, New York Times reported that the Mexican regime "is campaigning hard for an amendment to the Mexican Constitution that would allow Mexicans living in the United States to retain Mexican nationality rights even when they adopt American citizenship."

Like their supposed enemies in the radical Chicano movement, Mexican officials do not shy away from expressions of racial and ethnic solidarity with Hispanics residing in this country. During a speech to Mexican-American politicians in Dallas, Mexican President Ernesto Zedillo declared, "You're Mexicans—Mexicans who live north of the border." Jose Angel Gurria, Mexico's foreign minister, has explained that the "double nationality amendment [is] designed to stress our common language . . . culture, [and] history" across national borders. The proposed amendment is intended to create a political fifth column under the influence of the Mexican regime. As Rodolfo O. de la Garza, a professor of government at the University of Texas, observes, "As Mexican-Americans become more powerful, the Mexican government wants them to defend Mexican interests here in the United States."

VOTING RIGHTS FOR NONCITIZENS?

The next logical step would be to extend the voting franchise to immigrants who are not citizens—a possibility which is being openly discussed by open borders activists in California and elsewhere. Jorge Casteñada, an influential Mexican intellectual and a columnist for the Los Angeles Times, defends the idea in his book The Mexican Shock: Its Meaning for the U.S.:

> Immigration from Mexico is likely to continue regardless of what enthusiasts of free trade, peace in Central America, or the closing of the border may say or do. The only realistic way to alter the negative effect of Mexican influence on California, then, is to change the nature of its origin by legalizing immigration [that is, extending another amnesty to illegals] and giving foreigners the right to vote in state and local elections.

In his book Importing Revolution: Open Borders and the Radical Agenda, William Hawkins of the Hamilton Center for National Strategy observes, "Non-citizen voting for local government has already been implemented in the liberal suburban enclave of Tacoma Park, Maryland. . . . Nearby in Washington, DC, City Councilman Frank Smith has endorsed legislation to allow non-citizens to vote in local elections in the nation's capital." Jamin Raskin, a law professor at American University, has noted, "Increasingly, advocates for immigrants in New York—as in Washington, Los Angeles and several smaller cities across the nation—have begun exploring the sensitive issue of securing voting privileges for immigrants who are not citizens." Raskin insists that "noncitizen voting is the suffrage movement of the decade" and predicts:

> [I]f picked up by large cities—like Los Angeles, Washington, New York and Houston—it could strengthen American democracy by including in the crucial processes of local government many hundreds of thousands of people born elsewhere. . . . There are 10 million legal immigrants who are not United States citizens. In number, at least, they represent a potential political force of some diversity and dimension, particularly in such cities as New York.

THE "UN-MAKING" OF AMERICA

The enfranchisement of foreigners would lead to the literal "un-making" of America as a sovereign, independent nation. While such a prospect is presently shocking, it is not in principle significantly different from the logic of our post-1965 immigration policy. After all, if everyone has an unconditional "right" to come to America and feast at the welfare trough, why should there be any defining advantages to citizenship? Why not eliminate our borders altogether, and extend all of the rights and privileges of citizenship to anyone who happens to occupy our nation at any given time?

> "Hate crimes against gay people are at epidemic proportions today, inflamed by inappropriate anger about and fear of *AIDS*."

HOMOSEXUALS FACE SIGNIFICANT DISCRIMINATION

Brian McNaught

In the following viewpoint, Brian McNaught maintains that gays and lesbians face pervasive discrimination in the workplace. This discrimination, the author argues, stems from the attitudes, assumptions, and behaviors of coworkers and often makes it difficult for gay employees to be fully productive. McNaught concludes that eliminating antigay discrimination in the workplace requires that employers openly advocate tolerance and educate employees on gay issues. McNaught, a workplace consultant on gay, lesbian, and bisexual issues, has published and produced numerous educational materials on homosexuality and on AIDS. He is also the author of *On Being Gay* and *Gay Issues in the Workplace*, from which this viewpoint is taken.

As you read, consider the following questions:

1. What is heterosexism, according to McNaught?
2. In the author's opinion, what is the difference between heterosexism and homophobia?
3. According to McNaught, how are homophobia and sexism connected?

R on is out for dinner with his boss and male co-workers. During the meal, one of his colleagues interjects a joke he heard on the radio that morning.

"Do you know what G-A-Y stands for?" he asks with an inebriated grin. "Got AIDS yet?"

The others laugh, some nervously. Ron quickly assesses who told the joke, how the boss responded, and whether anyone refused to laugh.

At the end of the meal, the suggestion is made that they all head to the Kitkat Club for the last female strip show of the evening and a nightcap. It's the boys' night out. Why not?

Margaret is sitting with co-workers at lunch in the cafeteria. Beth asks if anyone saw that made-for-TV movie on the Fox channel the night before.

"What was it about?" asks Pam.

"It was about this gay kid who was supposed to get married and tried to kill himself."

"That stuff makes me sick," says Phyllis. "I hate all of this queer stuff. Pat Buchanan is right. Where will it stop?"

HETEROSEXISM AT WORK

What we see in these two stories is heterosexism at work. Heterosexism is the belief that everyone is heterosexual or ought to be.

Ron is a gay man. His lover of six years, Tom, is HIV-positive.

Margaret is a heterosexual woman. Her thirty-year-old daughter, Sally, recently told her that she is a lesbian.

Presuming that Ron is heterosexual, that he wouldn't be offended by the anti-gay joke, and that he would be interested in going to the heterosexual strip joint are examples of heterosexism.

Presuming that Margaret or anyone else at the table wouldn't be offended by a co-worker's disgust at gay people is also heterosexist. Phyllis made an assumption, and as Felix Unger of "The Odd Couple" aptly stated, "When we assume we make an *ass* of u and me."

When employers put *married* or *single* on application forms, they are assuming that all respondents are either heterosexually married or heterosexually single. When management decides to transfer Bill across the country because he's not married, they assume that there is no significant person in his life who will have to pull up stakes, change jobs, and relocate with him. That's heterosexism.

When the social committee states on the party invitations that employees are welcome to bring their families, they generally mean their heterosexual families—wife or husband and kids. When the boss asks Marilyn, because she's "single," to cover the office during the holiday so that the rest of the employees can be with their families, that too is heterosexism. It assumes heterosexually unmarried people have no family.

AN UNCONSCIOUS BIAS

Heterosexism is a worldview. For most people, it is probably not even conscious. It is a mind-set based upon limited opportunity to experience diversity. It is also a bias. Because we as individuals are proud to be who or what we are, we think everyone should be like us or, at the very least, should want to be like us.

I am guilty of having had such a bias. As a child, I naively thought all people were Catholic, and if they weren't, once they heard about the Church they would want to be. I recall feeling obliged to remind people that it was Friday, so they shouldn't be eating meat. Mom laughed with embarrassment (in later life) at how she would get phone calls from the neighbors who pleaded, "Virginia, please ask Brian not to try to convert our children to Catholicism."

As a young adult, I learned that not everyone was Catholic or believed what Catholics believed. Further, I learned to my surprise that not everyone liked Catholics. My worldview changed with information and experience. Realizing the existence of Jews, for instance, and respecting their right to believe differently, I became more cautious about my language, such as in not wishing everyone on the street "Merry Christmas" during the last couple weeks of December. It was easier when I thought everyone was a Catholic, but I realize now that I both excluded and offended a lot of people with my mind-set.

Heterosexism has the same effect. The truth is that not everyone is heterosexual. Most of the people who are not don't wish they were, and they value their relationships as intensely as most heterosexuals do. People who are not heterosexual also value their weekends, holidays, and other time away from work. They don't like it presumed they are heterosexual any more than people who are not Catholic like it presumed that they are.

HETEROSEXISM IN THE WORKPLACE

Heterosexism creates havoc in the workplace because it sends out the message that all employees should be heterosexual. For those readers who are heterosexual, imagine for a moment that you are gay and that I am your heterosexual office mate. If I assume that you are like me—heterosexual—I make it difficult for you to tell me that I am wrong. If it is difficult for you to tell me, you will keep your mouth shut and I will continue to assume. I will do things and say things that are inappropriate and sometimes offensive and you won't trust me. Because you have a secret you assume I don't want to hear, you don't feel comfortable with me and don't collaborate as much as you might. That makes it difficult for you to be fully productive and reduces the effectiveness of our teamwork.

SANCTIONS AGAINST HOMOSEXUALITY

American culture privileges sexual behavior that occurs in heterosexual marriage. For example, two people of the same gender cannot marry in the United States. Thus, they are excluded from many of the benefits of marriage, such as child custody and adoption, insurance benefits, and inheritance. In some cases, people may lose their jobs or homes by revealing that they are homosexual or bisexual. Only a few jurisdictions have laws prohibiting such discrimination, and some of these laws are currently under challenge. Furthermore, homosexuals or bisexuals may fear being stigmatized or rejected by coworkers or family members.

Charlene L. Muehlenhard, *SIECUS Report*, December 1995/January 1996.

As a manager, if I assume that everyone who works for me is a heterosexual person, I am less likely to be concerned about gay issues in the workplace; I am less aware of the toll of inappropriate comments on homosexuality; I am less inclined to think it worth the company's while to educate employees about gay and lesbian issues; I am less likely to use inclusive language; I am also less likely to hear from gay, lesbian, or bisexual employees about the difficulties they face in doing their job. That clearly would make me a less effective manager. . . .

THE HOMOPHOBIA CONTINUUM

Heterosexism is the assumption that everyone is heterosexual or ought to be. Homophobia is different. Homophobia is the fear and hatred of homosexuality in ourselves and/or in other people.

If you think of homophobia on a continuum, at one end we have the violent physical attacks against gay men and lesbian women. Hate crimes against gay people are at epidemic proportions today, inflamed by inappropriate anger about and fear of AIDS.

When I was Boston Mayor Kevin White's liaison to the gay and lesbian community, the mayor had me conduct a survey on constituent needs. Of the 1,600 people who responded to our questions, 76 percent reported they had been verbally assaulted for being gay and 24 percent said they had been physically assaulted because someone perceived they were gay. These alarming percentages have been repeated in study after study at city, state, and national levels.

Most often, the assailant is a male who victimizes gay men primarily with verbal assaults, beatings, and even murder. Some gay men are raped. Lesbian women are more often raped, and they are also victims of verbal abuse, beatings, and murder.

When I first began doing gay-issues work in corporate America, I would say, "But we aren't talking about violence in the workplace." Regrettably, however, today we *are* talking about this frightening end of the homophobia continuum being evidenced at work. In one corporation, several people associated publicly with the gay and lesbian employee support group have received death threats on their office telephone answering machines or in letters sent to both office and home. Threats are also made in bathroom graffiti or even, remarkably enough, face-to-face.

EXAMPLES OF HOMOPHOBIA

At the other end of the homophobia continuum, we have the occasional joke that someone tells at the lunchroom table, the offensive anti-gay cartoon taped to an office door, or the limp-wristed impersonation when talking about homosexuals.

The use of words like *fag, dyke, queer, fairy, pansy, lezzie,* and *homo* to belittle a person is homophobic. Jokes and comments about homosexuals that are negative and hostile are homophobic. Any effort to intimidate a person because the person is gay, perceived to be gay, or perceived to be supportive of gay people is homophobic.

Tony gets off the company's elevator and hears as the doors close, "I hope you die of AIDS." That's homophobia.

"So you like sex with girls? I'd like to have sex with you and another girl. Call me and we can get it on." That message from a man on Kathleen's office telephone answering machine is also an example of homophobia.

The wall in the office men's room states, "Do your part. Stop AIDS. Smash a fag. Say no to gay rights. Gay rights are the AIDS of society." Here, again, we have homophobia.

Signs with my picture, announcing to employees that I was the company's guest noon-hour speaker, have been defaced. Literature displayed by the gay employee support group has been torn up. The car in the employee parking lot belonging to the openly gay woman was vandalized with deep gouges. These are all instances of homophobia, too. . . .

SEXISM AND HOMOPHOBIA

I believe there is a clear link between sexism, heterosexism, and homophobia, particularly for men and women who feel personally threatened by homosexuality. Sexism is the belief that one gender is superior to the other. As most commonly experienced, sexism is the value that it is better to be male than female, that masculine characteristics have more status than feminine ones.

Within the larger Western culture, the degree of sexism varies according to race and ethnicity. The more sexist the culture or subculture, the more strictly defined and enforced are the gender roles. The more strictly defined and enforced the gender roles are, the more homophobic the culture or subculture will be.

If being male is best and being female is inferior, a "real man" is defined as one who is fully male, or, without female attributes. He "thinks" like a man, sharing interest with all other "real men" in such things as excelling in sports, earning a big salary, and being sexually dominant with women. He "acts" like a man, refusing to participate in any behavior thought to be the least bit feminine, such as cooking, doing dishes, nurturing a child, or crying. He "looks" like a man, preferring clothes, haircuts, and even modes of transportation that distinguish him from women.

If one values maleness in such a way and seeks, for the sake of security, membership in the powerful male community, one abhors anything that threatens that image. Homosexuals, particularly homosexual men, more specifically effeminate homosexual men, threaten that image.

Homosexual men are not thought by some heterosexual men to be "real men," thus such words and expressions as *fairy, sissy, pansy, shim, he/she, light in the loafers, poof, queen* are used to describe homosexual men. The very first time most boys pick up a ball, they hear, "Don't throw the ball like a girl" or "Don't throw the ball like a sissy," and the two become interchangeable; being a sissy is equal to being like a girl. Both homosexual and heterosexual men are raised to fear being called *sissy, little girl,* and *queer.* Homosexual men like being men. However, some homosexual men, as well as some heterosexual men, do not embrace every gender role deemed essential by culture to identify them as "real men." Some appear to be "sissies" or "like a girl." To the insecure heterosexual man, that can be very disturbing.

Lesbian women can be feared and hated by insecure men and

women for different reasons. Insecure heterosexual women can feel defensive toward lesbians because lesbians aren't perceived as buying into preconceived notions of what it means to be "real women." Insecure heterosexual men can be intimidated by what they perceive to be a lesbian's lack of need of them. Some people believe that "real women" need "real men."

ELIMINATING HOMOPHOBIA

Eliminating homophobia that is fueled by this insecurity is best achieved through contact with gay people, education, and the opportunity to talk about one's feelings. Education allows for the dismantling of the myths that exacerbate insecurities. Defensiveness is diminished when individuals no longer feel threatened. . . .

Homophobia, like racism, sexism, and anti-Semitism is not easily eliminated. People in the workplace are entitled to believe whatever they wish but should not be allowed to engage in behavior that creates a hostile environment for their colleagues. A strong company policy that prohibits discrimination is essential. So too is comprehensive education. But the most important ingredient is the determination of the company to recognize and resolve the problem.

To challenge heterosexism and to eliminate homophobic behaviors, managers have to be role models. Employers have to be consistent examples. Rather than delegate this responsibility to the human resource office, everyone in authority, from the CEO on down, needs to become an advocate for tolerance. Persons in positions of authority need to be ever mindful that whether they like it or not, they are constantly being watched and listened to by all employees for the appropriate way to behave in the workplace.

If a manager tolerates inappropriate comments about gay people, if he or she stays silent in the presence of homophobic behaviors, the corporate policy has no meaning in that particular work environment. If a manager provides training for his or her employees on gay issues but does not enthusiastically lead the effort to eliminate heterosexism and homophobia from the workplace, gay people will stay in the closet and continue to be less productive than they could be.

| "The dubious notion that gays are a powerless and victimized minority ... [is] belied by the facts."

HOMOSEXUALS DO NOT FACE SIGNIFICANT DISCRIMINATION

Justin Raimondo

In the following viewpoint, Justin Raimondo maintains that gays and lesbians do not face significant discrimination. According to Raimondo, homosexuals as a group have not demonstrated an inability to obtain wealth or political power because of prejudice against their sexual orientation. Furthermore, he contends, measures designed to prevent discrimination against homosexuals would actually grant them special favors and privileges while infringing on the rights of employers and organizations that support traditional moral standards. Raimondo is the author of *Coexistence or Culture War: What Does the Gay Lobby Want?*

As you read, consider the following questions:

1. What statistics does Raimondo cite to support his contention that homosexuals do not face economic discrimination?
2. Why did the United Way, Bank of America, and Levi Strauss initially withdraw their financial support from the San Francisco Bay Area chapter of the Boy Scouts, according to Raimondo?
3. How does the author define "heterophobia"?

From Justin Raimondo, "Let Markets, Not Laws, Correct Irrational Hiring," *Insight*, September 12, 1994. Reprinted by permission of *Insight* magazine. Copyright ©1994 by The Washington Times Corporation. All rights reserved.

The gay-rights movement is waging an all-out offensive against traditional culture, and its program, if enacted, would entail a massive violation of rights—the rights to property, free association and control of the moral education of one's children.

The movement's assault on liberty, the Employment Non-Discrimination Act of 1994, or ENDA, prohibiting workplace discrimination on the basis of sexual orientation [ENDA was defeated in the Senate in 1995], is founded on three myths promulgated by the gay lobby—three false premises that almost never are challenged. Underlying this mythology is the dubious notion that gays are a powerless and victimized minority—a posture of passivity belied by the facts.

ALLEGED DISCRIMINATION

Myth No. 1: *Gays are economically oppressed.* Statistics produced by market research studies tell a different story. Concentrated in the higher income brackets, in the arts and in the professional classes, gay male couples earn a combined average income of $51,325 a year; the average lesbian couple brings in $45,927. In 1990, average household income in the United States was $36,520. Not surprisingly, 48 percent of gay men and 43 percent of lesbians are homeowners. While the rationale for passing antidiscrimination laws used to be helping the poor, today we are faced with the absurdity of a movement demanding an end to alleged economic discrimination against the one demographic group with the most disposable income.

Gay-rights advocates claim that ENDA will not lead to special treatment under the aegis of affirmative action. But that is what Hubert Humphrey said in 1964, arguing for passage of the Civil Rights Act. Since the idea of discrimination is necessarily subjective and unknowable—unless government enforcers are mind-readers—the only way to measure it is by examining statistics. Such judgments are especially subjective when it comes to sexual orientation. As columnist Mona Charen put it: "Forbidding discrimination against gays is like forbidding discrimination against mystery readers—how does an employer know?"

Richard Tafel, national director of the gay Log Cabin Republicans, argues that ENDA reflects the ideas of those "who believe merit should be the sole basis for hiring." But the market economy automatically punishes irrational discrimination: In a most un-Republican manner, Tafel would replace market mechanisms with government regulations and give federal bureaucrats rather than employers the power to define standards of "merit."

Myth No. 2: *Gays can't help it, they were born that way.* This conception of gay people as a new kind of ethnic group is the central pillar of gay-rights mythology; it is what unites Bruce Bawer and Michelangelo Signorile, Act-Up [AIDS Coalition to Unleash Power] and the gay Republicans. With the growth of the gay subculture as a commercial and ideological enterprise, the subjective feeling that being homosexual was almost like being a member of a race hardened into a political dogma. Against the fact that homosexuality is a behavior and not a trait such as blue eyes or red hair, the ideologues of the gay movement had to construct a single overarching concept that would unify a great many diverse individuals. What they came up with was the idea of homosexuality as an intrinsic quality, not a behavior but a state of being, and more than that—an inheritable characteristic, genetically inscribed in every cell. Strangely, these very same people scream bloody murder whenever anyone attributes the behavior of other victim groups, such as women or blacks, to genetic factors.

The theory of intrinsic homosexuality is a fragile foundation upon which to build a movement, let alone a sense of self. For the inconvenient truth of the matter is that there is no scientific proof for the theory that homosexual behavior is genetically encoded. This lack of evidence, combined with a mass of cross-cultural data, strongly indicates that homosexuality is socially linked to the development of moral and esthetic values—and that, therefore, a large element of choice is involved.

THE INTOLERANCE OF THE GAY LOBBY

Myth No. 3: *The gay lobby is a movement of the oppressed and the powerless, a crusade for tolerance, diversity and libertarian values.* No one denies that the power of the state has been used as a bludgeon against gay people since at least the High Middle Ages. The great irony is that today, as tolerance of homosexuality seems to be growing, the leaders of the gay-rights movement seem to be saying, "Now it's our turn."

Their argument has by now become all too familiar: "We have been persecuted by the followers of an ascetic—and vengeful—desert god, and now we demand full status as an officially approved victim group, right up there with women, blacks and other U.S. government-approved minorities. And if the social mores will not yield to our assault, then we will use the battering ram of government power to storm the fortress and take the city. We are victims and now it is our turn."

To understand the political and cultural meaning of ENDA and the forces behind it, look at the early 1990s hate campaign unleashed against the San Francisco Bay–area chapter of the Boy Scouts. Leading the charge was Roberta Achtenberg, then on the San Francisco City Council but later brought to Washington by the Clinton administration to serve as undersecretary of the Department of Housing and Urban Development (HUD). While on the council, Achtenberg teamed up with fanatics on the school board to drive the Boy Scouts out of the city's public schools.

A COMPARISON OF GAY AND NATIONAL ECONOMIC SUCCESS

Category	Gay	National
Average annual household income	$55,430	$32,144
College graduates (%)	59.6	18.0
Professional/managerial positions (percentage of those working)	49.0	15.9
Overseas Travelers (1987)	65.8	14.0
Frequent Flyers (1987) (percentage taking 5 or more domestic flights)	26.5	1.9

Source: Simmons Market Research Bureau, 1988.

The anti-Scout campaign was supported by the president of San Francisco's school board, Tom Ammiano, a gay public-school teacher who moonlights as a professional comedian. The rationale behind his edict banning Boy Scout activities from school premises was that they "discriminate" against gay members and counselors. While this may sound like a sick joke—we are, after all, talking about mostly preteen boys here—in San Francisco such a lunatic idea was and is taken seriously, and "gays in the Boy Scouts" became a local cause. Under threat of economic and political retaliation, several important local companies withdrew their financial support from the Scouts: the United Way, Bank of America and Levi Strauss all joined the lynch mob, and the fanatics were deluded into thinking they had scored a victory.

THE BATTLE OF THE BOYCOTTS

Not so fast. Bank of America's phone was soon ringing off the hook, and the message came through loud and clear: Stop the attack on the Boy Scouts or face a boycott from irate parents. Ditto for Wells Fargo and Levi Strauss. Fifty members of Congress signed a letter denouncing the anti-Scouts campaign, and they weren't all Republicans. Democratic presidential candidate Bill

Clinton, touted by the gay lobby as their Abraham Lincoln, backed away from their embrace, stating that, as a private organization, the Scouts have the right to set their own membership criteria.

Under considerable pressure, Bank of America relented, restored funding to the Scouts—and immediately came under attack from groups who announced a boycott and threatened retaliation against any local politico who failed to go along. It was at this point that Achtenberg introduced legislation cutting back the extent of the city's dealings with Bank of America. Although Mayor Frank Jordan succeeded in deflecting the anti-Scout jihad, what is significant here is the unhesitating impulse of the gay movement to use government to further its own cultural and political agenda.

Subsidizing the Gay Agenda

The gay culture warriors use government not only to punish their perceived enemies, but also to subsidize their own. During her tenure on the city council, Achtenberg was instrumental in using part of a HUD grant to finance the Lavender Youth Recreation and Information Center, or LYRIC, to the tune of $500,000.

In fiscal year 1993, HUD granted $22,041,000 to San Francisco through its Community Development Bloc Grant, or CDBG, program. Since local communities are free to spend CDBG money any way they choose, Achtenberg simply exercised her political clout and managed to divert a good chunk of this money to LYRIC.

What is the purpose of LYRIC? The San Francisco *Independent* quotes LYRIC Director Dan Barutta: "Ever since we started this program, we decided that youth need a variety of things. A lot of the boys want a homey atmosphere where they can do homework and talk to older adults and hang out." Loaded with federal tax dollars, LYRIC is looking to buy a three-story Victorian in the heart of San Francisco's gay Castro district.

Destroy the Boy Scouts and create a government-funded gay youth program—what kind of an agenda is this? . . .

We hear much about "homophobia" these days. The gay lobby plays fast and loose with the term, using its clinical accusing tone. Very little is said, however, about the other phobia, the Phobia That Dares Not Speak Its Name.

Heterophobia

I refer, of course, to heterophobia: fear and loathing of heterosexuals.

We haven't heard very much about heterophobia for a couple

of reasons. To begin with, it took a while for heterophobia to rear its ugly head. After all, it wasn't that long ago that gay bars routinely were raided by the police. And not only bars, but also gay political organizations, were shut down. The first gay political group in the country, the Society for Human Rights, founded in Chicago in 1923, was closed down by police raids two years later. In fighting a strictly defensive war for nearly half a century, the gay movement was too busy surviving to think about going on the offensive. It took awhile before the idea of launching an all-out assault on straight society's most sacred institutions occurred to anyone. It was only after homosexuality had been thoroughly legitimized (and politicized), at least among the elite, that heterophobia was able to make any headway.

The Boy Scouts were singled out because there is no better symbol of middle-class American life and values. Here is a sacred symbol of all that is good and wholesome, the traditional American icon of virtuous male conduct—a perfect target for a schoolyard bully looking for a fight. The hate campaign against the Boy Scouts is emblematic of the heterophobic fervor that afflicts the gay-rights movement, for it occurred in a city where homosexuals, far from being a powerless and oppressed minority, are perhaps the single most influential factor in local politics. While unique in many respects, San Francisco serves as a kind of sociopolitical laboratory in which we can project what would happen if the gay-rights movement achieved its goals on a wide scale. . . .

GAY PRIDE?

In his book, *A Place at the Table: The Gay Individual in America*, gay neo-conservative Bawer repeatedly declares that what he wants is not to be tolerated but accepted. What he wants, he says, is a world "in which every heterosexual can look at a gay couple and say: 'What they feel for each other is a good thing. Let us rejoice in it.'"

Besides being unrealistic, this expectation is oddly contradictory. It is a perverse kind of "gay pride" that seeks the approval of others as a precondition for its own fulfillment. This question of endowing homosexuality with some sort of moral sanction, to be bestowed by official act of government, is what the fight over gay-rights legislation is really all about—not the merits of ENDA, but its symbolic meaning. Stamped with the moral imprimatur of government sanction, gays will be given their place at the table and served their fair share of government favors, special rights and subsidies.

ENDA would project the heterophobic agenda of the gay rights movement onto the national scene; it would put an end to private organizations, such as the Boy Scouts, that insist on setting their own moral standards. As such, it should be opposed by conservatives and all right-thinking people—of whatever sexual "orientation."

PERIODICAL BIBLIOGRAPHY

The following articles have been selected to supplement the diverse views presented in this chapter. Addresses are provided for periodicals not indexed in the *Readers' Guide to Periodical Literature*, the *Alternative Press Index*, the *Social Sciences Index*, or the *Index to Legal Periodicals and Books*.

Jeffrey Abramson	"Making the Law Colorblind," *New York Times*, October 16, 1995.
Robert L. Carter	"The Criminal Justice System Is Infected with Racism," *Vital Speeches of the Day*, March 1, 1996.
Mark Feldstein	"Hitting the Poor Where They Live," *Nation*, April 4, 1994.
Chad G. Glover	"Still Second-Class Citizens," *Essence*, September 1994.
Edward S. Herman	"America the Meritocracy," *Z Magazine*, July/August 1996.
Elizabeth Kadetsky	"Bashing Illegals in California," *Nation*, October 17, 1994.
E. Kuster	"'Lookism': The Work-Place's Dirty Little Secret," *Glamour*, September 1993.
John Leo	"Our Hypersensitive Society," *U.S. News & World Report*, July 4, 1994.
Nicolaus Mills	"Lifeboat Ethics and Immigration Fears," *Dissent*, Winter 1996.
New Republic	"Crossing the Line," February 19, 1996.
Patricia O'Toole	"The Contagion of Prejudice," *Glamour*, July 1995.
Janine S. Pouliot	"Rising Complaints of Religious Bias," *Nation's Business*, February 1996.
Jason L. Riley	"Don't Cry Wolf on Racism," *Wall Street Journal*, January 26, 1996.
J.S. Robb	"No Americans Need Apply," *National Review*, November 6, 1996.
Jeffrey Rosen	"Like Race, Like Gender?" *New Republic*, February 19, 1996.
Matthew Rothschild	"Get Up, Stand Up," *Progressive*, May 1996.

WHAT CAUSES
DISCRIMINATION?

CHAPTER PREFACE

In 1954, the U.S. Supreme Court declared school segregation unconstitutional, claiming that racially isolated schools produced a "feeling of inferiority" in and had "a tendency to retard the educational and mental development" of African American children. Supporters of desegregation argued that racially separate education was inherently unequal and that it kept deeply entrenched patterns of discrimination intact. Integrating public schools, they surmised, would be one step toward dismantling racial discrimination and promoting equal opportunity for black Americans.

More than forty years after the Supreme Court's decision, however, many educators are unhappy with the outcome of integrated education. Some black leaders contend that the desegregated public school actually fosters discrimination. For example, they argue, black children who are bused to schools in white neighborhoods often face negative racial stereotypes held by white students and teachers. White teachers who have lower expectations for African Americans cannot bring out the best in black students, critics maintain. According to CQ *Researcher* staff writer Kenneth Jost, black students in public schools are "twice as likely as whites to be placed in special-education classes but half as likely to enter classes for academically inclined students." Arguing that this lowered academic output is the result of teacher expectation rather than student ability, some black leaders advocate a return to racially separate neighborhood schools where black students would learn in a supportive, predominantly black environment.

On the other hand, supporters of desegregation maintain that minority children who attend desegregated schools have made significant gains. They argue that desegregated education has resulted in a thirty-point increase on Scholastic Achievement Test (SAT) scores among black students. More importantly, desegregation advocates claim, minority students who attend integrated schools raise their chances of attending the colleges of their choice and finding good jobs afterward. Minorities who attend desegregated schools are also more likely to live and work in integrated environments after they graduate, pro-integration advocates contend. They conclude that well-planned school desegregation is not a source of discrimination, but rather is a successful tool for dismantling discrimination.

School desegregation is just one of the topics debated in the following chapter in which commentators examine the causes of discrimination.

"*African Americans often experience hostility and mistreatment when they venture into spaces where many whites question the presence of a black person.*"

RACISM CAUSES DISCRIMINATION

Joe R. Feagin and Melvin P. Sikes

Blacks' experiences of mistreatment at public accommodations is due to white racism, contend Joe R. Feagin and Melvin P. Sikes in the following viewpoint. Though civil rights laws legally require nondiscriminatory treatment of minorities, the authors maintain, African Americans continue to face overt discrimination from whites at restaurants, stores, hotels, and other public places. This discrimination, Feagin and Sikes argue, is rooted in a racist mindset that developed early in America's history. Feagin and Sikes are the authors of Living with Racism: The Black Middle-Class Experience, from which this viewpoint is excerpted.

As you read, consider the following questions:

1. According to Feagin and Sikes, what kind of discriminatory treatment have African Americans faced at some national-chain restaurants?
2. Why do whites often accuse blacks of being "racially paranoid," in the authors' opinion?
3. How do the media affect public perceptions of black-on-white crime, according to the authors?

Title II of the most important civil rights act of the twentieth century, the 1964 Civil Rights Act, stipulates that "all persons shall be entitled to the full and equal enjoyment of the goods, services, facilities, privileges, advantages, and accommodations of any place of public accommodation . . . without discrimination or segregation on the ground of race, color, religion, or national origin." Yet, as we approach the twenty-first century, this promise of full and equal enjoyment of the public places and accommodations of the United States is far from reality for African Americans.

Not long ago Debbie Allen, a movie-star and television producer, recounted a painful experience with discrimination at a Beverly Hills jewelry store. A white clerk, possibly stereotyping Allen as poor or criminal, refused to show her some jewelry. Allen was so incensed that she used the incident as the basis for an episode on a television show. Across the country in Tamarac, Florida, a twenty-year-old black man, wearing a Syracuse University cap and hoping to invest his savings, visited a branch of Great Western Bank seeking information. After stopping at other banks, he returned to Great Western, got more information, and then went to his car to review the materials. There he was surrounded by sheriff's deputies with guns drawn, handcuffed, and read his rights. The deputies questioned him for some time before dismissing the report of white bank employees that the black man looked like a bank robber.

In this viewpoint, the middle-class respondents challenge us to reflect on their experiences with discrimination as they move into traditionally white public accommodations, such as upscale restaurants and department stores, and through public streets once the territory only of whites. They frequently report that their middle-class resources and status provide little protection against overt discrimination. Although there are, at least in principle, some social restraints on hostile white behavior in public accommodations, African Americans often experience hostility and mistreatment when they venture into spaces where many whites question the presence of a black person. . . .

DISCRIMINATION IN RESTAURANTS

That discrimination against black customers and employees in white-owned restaurants is widespread has become evident in several court suits filed since 1990 against national chains, including Denny's, Shoney's, and the International House of Pancakes (IHOP). In December 1991, for example, several groups of black college students were reportedly turned away from a

Milwaukee IHOP restaurant and told that it was closed, while white customers were allowed in. In 1993 a federal judge ordered the restaurant to pay a settlement for the discrimination. Also in 1993, the Denny's chain, found to have a pattern of discrimination by the U.S. Justice Department, reached an agreement with the Department in which executives promised to train employees in nondiscriminatory behavior and to include more minorities in its advertising. This settlement did not affect a class-action discrimination suit by thirty-two black customers who reportedly had suffered discrimination in several Denny's restaurants in California. Moreover, in mid-1993 six black secret service agents also sued the chain, alleging discrimination at a Denny's in Annapolis, Maryland. The black agents reported that while they waited for service for nearly an hour, white agents and other white patrons were promptly served. After much bad publicity, Denny's joined in an important agreement with the NAACP [National Association for the Advancement of Colored People] to work to end discrimination in its restaurants.

As revealed in the court cases, restaurant discrimination has recently included long waits while whites are served, special cover fees applied only to blacks, and prepayment requirements only for black customers. In the Shoney's case, the chain was sued over discrimination against black employees. According to the *St. Petersburg Times*, top officers in the white-run firm were well-known for their antiblack views, and local managers were discouraged from hiring black employees. In a 1992 landmark agreement the company agreed to pay $115 million, the most ever, to employees who could prove racial discrimination.

Restaurants are only one site of discrimination. . . .

DISCRIMINATION IN RETAIL STORES

Another problem that black customers face, especially in department and grocery stores, is the common white assumption that they are likely shoplifters. This is true in spite of the fact that national crime statistics show that most shoplifters are white. For several months in late 1991 a news team at KSTP-TV in Minneapolis conducted a field study of discrimination against black shoppers in several local department stores. Members of the team took jobs as security personnel in the stores, and black and white shoppers were sent into the stores in order to observe the reactions of white security personnel. The ensuing television report, "Who's Minding the Store?" showed how many black customers became the targets of intensive surveillance from white security guards, who neglected white shoppers when black shoppers were in the stores. As a result of the documentary, local black leaders called for a boycott of one of the store chains. Soon a number of the local stores changed their surveillance and security procedures. . . .

Among several respondents who discussed discrimination at retail stores, the manager of a career development organization, who found that discrimination by clerks is common, had a repertoire of responses for dealing with it:

> If you're in a store—and let's say the person behind the counter is white—and you walk up to the counter, and a white person walks up to the counter, and you know you were there before the white customer, the person behind the counter knows you were there first, and it never fails, they always go, "Who's next." Ok. And what I've done, if they go ahead and serve the white person first, then I will immediately say, "Excuse me, I was here first, and we both know I was here first.". . . If they get away with it once, they're going to get away with it more than once, and then it's going to become something else. And you want to make sure that folks know that you're not being naive, that you really see through what's happening. Or if it's a job opportunity or something like that, too, same thing. You first try to get a clear assessment of what's really going on and sift through that information, and then . . . go from there.

In discussions with middle-class black Americans across the nation, both our respondents and a variety of informants and journalists, we heard many similar accounts of white clerks "looking through" black customers and only "seeing" whites farther back in line. Such incidents suggest that much of the hostility manifest in white actions is based on a deep lying, perhaps even subconscious or half-conscious, aversion to black color and persona. This executive also spoke of her coping process, one that begins with sifting information before deciding on action. Frequently choosing immediate action, she forces whites to face the reality of their behavior.

PUBLIC MISTREATMENT

The dean of a black college who travels in various parts of the United States described the often complex process of evaluating and responding to the mistreatment that has plagued him in public accommodations:

> When you're in a restaurant and . . . you notice that blacks get seated near the kitchen. You notice that if it's a hotel, your room is near the elevator, or your room is always way down in a corner somewhere. You find that you are getting the undesirable rooms. And you come there early in the day and you don't see

very many cars on the lot and they'll tell you that this is all we've got. Or you get the room that's got a bad television set. You know that you're being discriminated against. And of course you have to act accordingly. You have to tell them, "Okay, the room is fine, [but] this television set has got to go. Bring me another television set." So in my personal experience, I simply cannot sit and let them get away with it and not let them know that I know that that's what they are doing. . . .

When I face discrimination, first I take a long look at myself and try to determine whether or not I am seeing what I think I'm seeing in 1989, and if it's something that I have an option [about]. In other words, if I'm at a store making a purchase, I'll simply walk away from it. If it's at a restaurant where I'm not getting good service, I first of all let the people know that I'm not getting good service, then I [may] walk away from it. But the thing that I have to do is to let people know that I know that I'm being singled out for separate treatment. And then I might react in any number of ways—depending on where I am and how badly I want whatever it is that I'm there for.

These recurring incidents in public accommodations illustrate the cumulative nature of discrimination. The dean first takes care to assess the incident and avoid jumping to conclusions. One must be constantly prepared on everyday excursions to assess accurately what is happening and then to decide on an appropriate response. What is less obvious here is the degree of pain and emotional drain that such a constant defensive stance involves.

WHITES OFTEN DISCOUNT BLACKS' COMPLAINTS
Whether some of the incidents reported by the last two respondents are in fact discriminatory is a question raised by some whites to whom we have shown these commentaries. Several have said that accounts of not being served in turn or being assigned poor hotel rooms are not necessarily racial discrimination, for whites too occasionally suffer such treatment. This raises the issue of how black accounts of discrimination are credited by whites. When we have discussed these accounts with black informants and journalists, they credit them quickly because of their own similar experiences. Years of cumulative experience give these middle-class black Americans the "second eye" that one respondent described, the ability to sense prejudice or discrimination even in a tone of voice, a look, or a gesture. Having occasionally experienced poor service themselves, however, many whites accuse blacks of being paranoid in seeing racism in such incidents. Yet it is the consistent pattern of bad

treatment, not only of oneself but of one's relatives and friends, by whites that is the basis for the black victims' interpretation of a particular incident as probable racial discrimination. Yet one more aspect of the burden of being black is having to defend one's understanding of events to white acquaintances without being labelled as racially paranoid.

BLACKS FACE DISCRIMINATION FROM POLICE

The typical white police officer holds all blacks in suspicion and treats them in a manner that constantly threatens their dignity and most basic rights. In some urban communities this amounts to life under a virtual police state for many law-abiding working-class and poor black Americans. Middle-class status makes some difference, but only in well-defined social situations. It can sometimes even be a disadvantage. . . . Every bourgeois black person [knows] that in unprotected contexts—driving on the highway, visiting a white suburban friend or caught in some minor traffic or other infraction—they are likely to find themselves specially targeted by white police officers and detectives who resent their success and take malignant pleasure in harassing them, especially if they are in mixed relationships.

Orlando Patterson, *New Republic*, November 6, 1995.

Many incidents in public accommodations have no ambiguity whatever. In many a white mind a black person standing in certain places is assumed to be in a menial position. A physician in an eastern state described her feelings when she was staying in nice hotels: "I hate it when you go places and [white] people . . . think that we work in housekeeping. . . . A lot of white people think that blacks are just here to serve them. And we have not risen above the servant position." Middle-class blacks report this experience of being taken by whites to be in servile positions. Even Democratic party presidential candidate Jesse Jackson had such an experience. Elegantly dressed and standing by an elevator in an upscale New York hotel, right after a meeting with an African political leader, Jackson was approached by a white woman who said "I couldn't have made it downstairs without you." She put a dollar in his hand, mistaking Jackson for her black bellhop. . . .

THE CUMULATIVE IMPACT OF DISCRIMINATION

The cumulative impact of several of these types of [public-place] discrimination was underscored by a black student at a large, mostly white university in the Southwest. He described his experiences walking home at night from a campus job to his apartment located in a predominantly white residential area:

So, even if you wanted to, it's difficult just to live a life where you don't come into conflict with others. Because every day you walk the streets, it's not even like once a week, once a month. It's every day you walk the streets. Every day that you live as a black person you're reminded how you're perceived in society. You walk the streets at night; white people cross the streets. I've seen white couples and individuals dart in front of cars to not be on the same side of the street. Just the other day, I was walking down the street, and this white female with a child, I saw her pass a young white male about twenty yards ahead. When she saw me, she quickly dragged the child and herself across the busy street. What is so funny is that this area has had an unknown *white* rapist in the area for about four years. [When I pass] white men tighten their grip on their women. I've seen people turn around and seem like they're going to take blows from me. The police constantly make circles around me as I walk home, you know, for blocks. I'll walk, and they'll turn a block. And they'll come around me just to make sure, to find out where I'm going. So, every day you realize [you're black]. Even though you're not doing anything wrong; you're just existing. You're just a person. But you're a black person perceived in an unblack world.

In a subsequent comment this student described how white men had hurled objects and racist epithets at him as he walked home. Discrimination is every day and everywhere. This student's experience is an example of what Ralph Ellison meant when he wrote of the general white inability to "see" black Americans as individuals in *Invisible Man*. Unable to perceive this black male student's middle-class symbols of college dress and books, white individuals and couples have crossed the street, dodging cars, to avoid walking near this medium-stature black student. They are doubtless reacting to the negative image of black males. The student perceives such avoidance in a particular instance as racially motivated, because he and his male friends have often encountered whites taking similar "defensive" measures.

STEREOTYPED VIEWS

The common white view of black men as dangerous, held by police and civilian whites alike, is deeply rooted in the history and collective psyche of white Americans. In a pathbreaking book, *The Black Image in the White Mind*, historian George Fredrickson has demonstrated that long before the twentieth century whites had developed a view of black slaves and servants as fearful and dangerous "beasts," a stereotyped view that has often lain behind white violence such as lynchings of black men. Still, this view persists. Today not just white police officers but many white media producers and commentators, and a majority of whites generally, appear to view criminals who commit violent crimes against white individuals and property to be mostly black or minority males. Yet the world of crime is complex and for the most part does not fit this white image. Most (78–88 percent) of the whites who are assaulted, raped, or murdered are attacked by white assailants, according to the 1991 National Crime Victimization Survey and other government crime data. While black assailants do account for 44 percent of the assailants of white robbery victims, they account for only 17 percent of the assailants in all crimes of violence targeting white victims.

BIAS IN THE MEDIA

In the white world black men, especially young black men, routinely suffer physical or psychological attacks from whites, yet such attacks get little publicity in the mass media, and then only when they are sensational. Attacks on whites by black men get much more media attention. For example, in a 1993 column about hate crimes and the First Amendment, nationally syndicated columnist James Kilpatrick focused only on one case, a racially motivated "get the white boy" attack on a white youth by some black teenagers. What is striking here is that such flagrant black-on-white cases are much less frequent than the reverse, today and even more so in the past, yet this prominent columnist did not find those white-on-black cases sufficiently newsworthy for his column. The case of "Willie" Horton, a black man who raped a white woman, is a celebrated example of the same biased focus on black-on-white crime. In 1988 the George Bush campaign used Horton's image to frighten white voters. Although the overwhelming majority of the rapists who attack white women are white, the negative image of the black man as a rapist of white women is so exaggerated and commonplace among white Americans that the campaign could make use of it to attract white voters to a conservative cause. Significantly, much media discussion and some scholarly dialogue have been devoted to white perceptions of black men as threatening and the justifiability of that perception. To our knowledge there has been no serious research or reporting on the very negative impact on the everyday lives of black men of white assumptions and the resulting avoidance and fear.

A SEVERE PROBLEM

Representing what appears to be a widely accepted view, one otherwise perceptive white analyst of discrimination has commented that whites' crossing the street to avoid black men is "a minimal slight." This is far from the truth. The black student quoted above reported that repeatedly being treated as a pariah, in his own words a "criminal and a rapist," has caused him severe psychological problems. Similarly, after a phone interview with the first author on some of this research on public-place discrimination, one of the nation's leading black journalists reported that middle-class whites sometimes stop talking—and white women grab their purses—when he enters an office-building elevator in his New England city. Whereas the student said that he rarely had been able to respond to the street encounters, apart from the occasional quick curse, because they happened too quickly, the journalist noted that when possible he has reacted more assertively; he described how he turns to whites in elevators and informs them, often with a smile, that they can continue talking or that he is not interested in their purses.

The NRC [National Research Council] report *A Common Destiny* found that by the late 1970s many whites believed that the Civil Rights Act of 1964 had brought a broad-scale elimination of racial discrimination in public accommodations. Robert Lauer and Warren Handel have written that as black Americans get access to an outer circle "from which they had been previously excluded (such as eating at a public restaurant) they encounter inner circles from which they are still excluded (such as equal access to economic opportunities) and with an even greater hostility than that with which they were barred from the outer circles." Unfortunately, our interviews and other sources indicate that deprivation of the full enjoyment of public facilities promised by the 1964 Civil Rights Act is not something of the past; attack, exclusion, rejection, and other types of antiblack discrimination persist in public accommodations today for African Americans, whatever their socioeconomic status. Streets and public accommodations are relatively unprotected sites, and African Americans are very vulnerable there to white maltreatment.

> "Are people who discriminate against people of other races by definition racist? Might prejudices reflect not ignorant predisposition but prudent judgment?"

RACISM IS NOT ALWAYS THE CAUSE OF DISCRIMINATION

Dinesh D'Souza

In the following viewpoint, Dinesh D'Souza contends that not all discrimination stems from racism. Instead, he argues, discrimination is often based on rational or commonsense assumptions about a person's appearance. Such "rational discrimination" may be based in part on a person's race but also takes into account other factors such as age, clothing, or behavior, D'Souza maintains. For example, he argues, cabdrivers who refuse to give rides to young black males may be discriminating not because of bigotry against African Americans but because of a rational fear based on the high percentage of young black criminals. The author of *The End of Racism*, D'Souza is also John M. Olin Scholar at the American Enterprise Institute, a conservative think tank.

As you read, consider the following questions:

1. According to D'Souza, why are current civil rights policies outdated?
2. Why do many minority groups feel more hostility to other ethnicities than whites do, in the author's opinion?
3. How does D'Souza define racism?

From Dinesh D'Souza, "Myth of the Racist Cabbie," *National Review*, October 9, 1995; ©1995 by National Review, Inc., 150 E. 35th St., New York, NY 10016. Reprinted with permission.

A generation after the civil-rights movement, Americans are once again engaged in a radical rethinking of their attitudes toward race. Racial preferences are now opposed by the vast majority of Americans; even among blacks, there is a new and vibrant diversity of opinion on the subject. Yet so far no one has questioned the very premises of the discussion. The basic assumption of our current racial debate is still that racism is the theory and discrimination is the practice. Racism is said to be based on "prejudices," which constitute judgments made in the absence of evidence, and "stereotypes," which are grossly misleading generalizations about groups. The obvious solutions, promoted by Martin Luther King and other activists, were twofold: statutes intended to outlaw racial discrimination, and social and educational programs to increase interaction between groups. As whites regularly lived and worked with blacks, their attitudes and actions toward them were expected to undergo a transformation, as ignorant prejudices gave way to enlightened acceptance.

As a result of these policies, state-sponsored segregation is dead; overt and arbitrary racial discrimination has greatly abated; white attitudes have undergone a revolutionary transformation in favor of equal rights in employment, housing, voting, and education; and there is a large and thriving black middle class. Yet, at the same time, the prevailing civil-rights model, and the laws and policies based on it, now seem irrelevant to contemporary problems, such as the lurid sufferings of the underclass, which have worsened over the past few decades. Consequently the debate seems to have been polarized and stalled by the crosscurrents of white backlash, black rage, and liberal despair. African-American scholar Derrick Bell conveys some of the regnant [widespread] frustration: "We have made progress in everything, yet nothing has changed."

Perhaps one way to gain an enlarged perspective on our current situation is to step back and turn our assumptions into questions. Are there circumstances in which discrimination actually makes sense? Are people who discriminate against people of other races by definition racist? Might prejudices reflect not ignorant predisposition but prudent judgment?

DISCRIMINATION AMONG CABDRIVERS

The problems with the prevailing civil-rights paradigm become evident when we examine the most widely cited contemporary example of racial discrimination—the refusal of many taxidrivers to pick up young African-American males. In a June

1993 article, Gregory Wright commented in the *Washington Post*:

> As an African American, I am fed up with having to flag down five cabs before finding one that will take me home, fed up with feeling anger, embarrassment, and frustration when cabdrivers swear they are off-duty and then pick up a white customer before I can get around the corner. Taxidrivers, many of whom come from Africa, the Caribbean, and the Middle East, say they don't want to pick up African-American passengers because they are afraid of being robbed, assaulted, or murdered. One Nigerian cabdriver told me he only picks up African Americans who are well dressed and look like businessmen. For African Americans, this discrimination can be inconvenient and downright humiliating.

It is easy to sympathize with the indignation expressed at such flagrant acts of racial discrimination. Yet according to Wright's own account, many of the cabdrivers who are reluctant to pick up young African-American males are themselves African, Caribbean, or Middle Eastern. Moreover, the Nigerian cited by Wright says explicitly that he will pick up blacks who are suitably dressed. His discrimination seems to be based not simply on skin color but on other aspects of appearance.

THE MYTH OF THE RACIST CABBIE

During my travels I took up the issue with a number of taxidrivers in New York, Washington, Chicago, and other cities. Most of them denied that they refuse to pick up every black male, and all ridiculed the notion that cabdrivers pass up black women. But many groused that African-American passengers frequently leave no tip and sometimes beat the fare, and virtually all acknowledged that as a consequence of previous threats, robberies, and assaults they employ a kind of heightened scrutiny before they will stop for a young black man.

"This racism stuff is all bull——," one African student who was driving to put himself through school told me. "I'm not going to pass up a fare, which is money in my pocket. But I don't want to get robbed. You know what the black crime rate is in New York? Do you want me to risk a gun to my head, man? What's wrong with you?" A white driver in Chicago told me, "No exceptions, pal. I never pick up niggers." "You don't like blacks?" I asked. "Not blacks. Niggers." "That sounds like racism to me." "Hey, that's c——. I pick up older blacks all the time. I have no problem with giving black women a ride. My black buddies won't pick up no niggers. I ain't no more racist than they are."

These concerns seem to be borne out by cabdriver muggings and killings. In August 1994, Keith Moore, a 38-year-old cabdriver and single father, was found with the keys in the ignition and two bullet wounds in his head. His friends told the *Washington Post* that he never worried about picking up passengers in questionable neighborhoods no matter what the time of day. If Moore had exercised prudence, his colleague Louis Richardson said, he probably would be alive today. The U.S. Labor Department has reported that driving a cab is the riskiest job in America, with occupational homicide rates higher than those for bartenders, gas-station attendants, and policemen.

These facts suggest how hollow it sounds to accuse cabdrivers of "prejudice" and "stereotypes." While we can be sure that racist taxidrivers would discriminate, not all taxidrivers who discriminate are racist.

RATIONAL DISCRIMINATION

Michelle Joo, an Asian-American shopkeeper in Washington, D.C., acknowledges that she discriminates based on race. When deciding whether to let people into her jewelry and cosmetics store, she tells the *Washington Post*, "I look at the face." She won't open the door "if he looks ugly, if he's holding a bottle in a paper bag, if he's dirty. . . . If some guy looks kind, I let him in." Young black men are kept out if they seem rowdy, Miss Joo says. Usually they react by banging on her glass windows. One may say that Michelle Joo has no fixed policy of keeping blacks out. Nor does she have a quota about the number she will admit. Rather, she seems to be a prudent statistician. She employs race as one factor, but not the only factor, in her decision-making. As a means to ensure her security and business survival, she is practicing what may be termed rational discrimination.

Thousands of other store owners in major cities make similar decisions every day. So do countless women—black, white, Hispanic, and Asian—who come across black males in circumstances they consider not entirely safe. Regardless of their general attitudes about civil rights, they do what they feel is necessary in each particular case. Shopkeepers scurry to the front of the store where they can monitor the exit. Female pedestrians may clutch their purse more tightly or cross the street if approached by one or more young black men. Sometimes people snap the locks on their car doors as African-American youths walk by.

The psychological toll of such reactions is high. If you are black, columnist William Raspberry says, it is unusual to find yourself treated as an individual, and to receive the kind of consideration that whites expect. In *The Rage of a Privileged Class*, Ellis Cose describes a typical justification for black rage: "Why am I constantly treated as if I were a drug addict, a thief, or a thug?" Many who echo these sentiments also question the basis for group judgments about blacks. Legal scholar Charles Ogletree argues that "99 per cent of black people don't commit crimes."

SOME PREJUDICE IS WARRANTED

Blacks make up approximately 12 per cent of the nation's population. Yet according to Uniform Crime Reports, published annually by the FBI, blacks account for 39 per cent of those arrested for aggravated assault, 42 per cent of those arrested for weapons possession, 43 per cent of those arrested for rape, 55 per cent of those arrested for murder, and 61 per cent of those arrested for robbery. Even discounting for the possibility of some racial bias in criminal arrests, it seems clear that the average black person is between three and six times as likely to be arrested for a crime as the average white person. . . .

Personally I would be angry and upset if, as a law-abiding person, I were routinely treated as a criminal by taxidrivers, storekeepers, or pedestrians. Yet, equally predictably, taxidrivers, storekeepers, and women who clutch their purses or cross the street will attach little significance to such personal and historical sensitivities. Such people are unlikely to be intimidated by accusations of prejudice. For them, the charges are meaningless, because the prejudice is warranted. In this context, a bigot is simply a sociologist without credentials.

THE LIBERAL UNDERSTANDING OF RACISM

It is now time to examine with fresh eyes the meaning of familiar terms such as prejudice and stereotype, which underlie the conventional liberal understanding of racism. African-American scholar Henry Louis Gates writes: "Racism exists when one generalizes about attributes of an individual, and treats him or her accordingly." Gates offers some specific examples: "You people sure can dance," and "Black people play basketball so remarkably well." He concludes, "These are racist statements." But are they?

In his classic work, *The Nature of Prejudice*, published in 1954, Gordon Allport drew on modern social-science theories to explicate the paradigm of liberal anti-racism. Allport argued that prejudices and stereotypes reveal less about their objects than their subjects. Applying such concepts as displacement and frustration-aggression theory, Allport maintained that when people feel hostility and anger which they have difficulty coping with, they project it onto others, who thus become sacrificial victims or "scapegoats." Allport helped to establish a premise that many social scientists continue to hold today: prejudices and stereotypes endure because of the principle of self-selection. From the distorted perspective of the racist, blacks who do not conform to preconceived notions simply do not exist; they are, in Ralph Ellison's term, invisible men.

REASONABLE DISCRIMINATION

Middle-class Americans, both white and black, see nothing wrong in discriminating against people whose behavior and values they find abhorrent, whatever their color. It is difficult to provide reasons why they should not discriminate on such grounds. Of course, most white Americans can and do distinguish between middle-class blacks and underclass blacks, but in so doing they must ignore those who would deny such distinctions. Among those who do so are black leaders and their white supporters who argue that there is nothing problematic about the behavior of the black underclass and who claim that whites are incapable of making distinctions among blacks due to endemic racism. The point is that denying the distinction between middle-class blacks and those in the underclass does not eliminate that distinction and, even more importantly, does nothing to improve the conditions in the inner cities.

Byron M. Roth, *Prescription for Failure*, 1994.

For the better part of a generation, this liberal understanding of racism worked fairly well. The reason was that both whites and blacks had indeed developed many erroneous views about each other as a consequence of the social isolation produced by Southern segregation. During slavery the races stayed in regular, even intimate, contact, but after emancipation the forced separation of the races created a divided society in which dubious and even absurd generalizations could endure, unchecked by contrary experience. The civil-rights movement's assault on prejudices and stereotypes, as well as the experience of desegregation, helped to topple many such group generalizations that could not withstand empirical examination.

JUDGMENTS ABOUT OTHER GROUPS

The problem with the liberal paradigm is its premise that *all* group perceptions are misperceptions. Paradoxically it is desegregation and integration which have called the liberal view into question. One of the risks of increased exposure to blacks is that it has placed whites in a position to discover which of their preconceived views are true.

In fact ethnic groups which have had little history of oppressing each other now seem to be formulating clear and often critical images of other groups. In one of the more remarkable surveys of recent years, the National Conference of Christians and Jews reports that many minority groups harbor much more hostile attitudes toward other minority groups than whites do. For example, 49 per cent of blacks and 68 per cent of Asians said that Hispanics "tend to have bigger families than they can support." Forty-six per cent of Hispanics and 42 per cent of blacks agreed that Asian Americans are "unscrupulous, crafty, and devious in business." And 53 per cent of Asians and 51 per cent of Hispanics affirmed that blacks "are more likely to commit crimes and violence."

It is, of course, possible that these minority perceptions reveal that, by a kind of social osmosis, everyone is learning racism from whites. But if so, why would minority perceptions be stronger than those of whites who are the alleged racists par excellence? More likely, these intergroup minority perceptions are the product of experience. Most people today have fairly regular contact with others of different races, and have many opportunities to verify their collective judgments about other groups.

PEOPLE'S PERCEPTION OF GROUP TRAITS

During my speaking trips to college campuses, I decided, as a journalistic exercise, to test people's perception of group traits by raising the question of whether stereotypes may be true and prejudices based on them therefore legitimate. Inevitably, I encountered strong emotional opposition. Educated people today have been taught to despise group generalizations. In a sense, we have been raised to be prejudiced against prejudice.

On a West Coast campus, I raised the question of whether, as a group, "blacks have rhythm." A professor of Afro-American Studies insisted, "Absolutely not," and a number of white students readily agreed. Instinctively, they raised the familiar defenses, "I know a black man who can't dance." "How can you generalize about a group that is so diverse?" "What about Elvis? He had rhythm, and he wasn't black," and so on. I pointed out that these were poor refutations of a proposition that was being offered as true on average, or compared with the experience of other groups. One cannot rebut the statistically irrefutable statement that men on average are taller than women by producing a six-foot woman and a four-foot man. Those individuals would merely constitute exceptions to a general pattern that has persisted across cultures for most of recorded history.

Incidentally, the view that blacks tend to be more rhythmic than whites is no whimsical recent invention but is supported by observation and experience in several cultures over two millennia. In ancient Greece and Rome, which held no negative view of black skin color, Ethiopians and other blacks were celebrated for a perceived natural inclination to music and dance. This is a central theme of that segment of Greek and Roman art which focuses on blacks. Moreover, the same perception of blacks is evident in many Arab descriptions of African blacks written in the late Middle Ages. Ibn Butlan, for example, writes that if a black man was dropped from heaven "he would beat time as he goes down." The Muslim historian Ibn Khaldun attributed the black African proclivity for music to the relaxing influence of the sun's heat.

On one point the liberal paradigm about group generalizations is sound: people's perceptions of others are always filtered through the lens of their own prior experience. But the liberal understanding cannot explain how particular traits come to be identified with particular groups. Only because group traits have an empirical basis in shared experience can we invoke them without fear of serious contradiction. Think how people would react if someone said, "Koreans are lazy," or "Hispanics are constantly trying to find ways to make money." Despite the prevalence of anti-Semitism, Jews are rarely accused of stupidity. Blacks are never accused of being tight with a dollar, or of conspiring to take over the world. By reversing stereotypes we can see how their persistence relies, not simply on the assumptions of the viewer, but also on the characteristics of the group being described.

STEREOTYPES CAN BE NEGATIVE OR POSITIVE

This is no case for group traits having a biological foundation. Probably the vast majority of group traits are entirely cultural, the distilled product of many years of shared experience. Yet prejudices and stereotypes are not intended to explain the origins of group traits, only to take into account their existence. Nor is this an argument to emphasize negative traits. Stereotypes can be negative or positive. Indeed the same stereotype can be interpreted favorably or unfavorably. One can deplore Roman machismo or admire Roman manliness; deride Spanish superstition or exalt Spanish piety; ridicule English severity or cherish English self-control. In each of these interpretations, we see a single set of facts, a different set of values.

William Helmreich, in *The Things They Say Behind Your Back*, takes up the issue of whether there is a rational basis for group stereotypes. Helmreich finds some stereotypes that are clearly false. During the Middle Ages, for example, apparently many Christians took religious polemic literally and came to believe that Jews have horns. Clearly this was not a perception destined to last: one has only to encounter a few Jews to discover that they do not, in fact, possess horns.

Helmreich takes up other stereotypes, however, such as the view that many Nobel laureates are Jewish, or that the Mafia is largely made up of Italians, or that the Japanese tend to be xenophobic and nationalistic, or that many Irishmen and American Indians drink enormous quantities of alcohol. Basically Helmreich finds that these perceptions are confirmed by the data. Of all the stereotypes he considers, Helmreich concludes that "almost half the stereotypes have a strong factual basis.". . .

Is discrimination based on race necessarily racist? Not if you define racism as a doctrine of intrinsic superiority and inferiority, which leads to judgments against a group on grounds of biology rather than conduct. Indeed, the existence of rational discrimination compels us to revise the liberal paradigm which holds that racism is the theory and discrimination is the practice. The two may be unconnected. It is possible to be a racist and not discriminate: this would be true of many poor and marginalized whites who might hate blacks and consider them inferior, but who are not in a position to enforce their convictions. So too it is possible to discriminate and not be a racist.

| "Racial stratification and separation permeate the integrated school."

INTEGRATED EDUCATION FOSTERS DISCRIMINATION

Doris Y. Wilkinson

In the following viewpoint, Doris Y. Wilkinson argues that legally enforced public school integration has resulted in increased discrimination against African American students. Citing the observations of two experienced teachers who work at desegregated schools, Wilkinson asserts that integration creates racially divisive school environments. These integrated schools do not meet the academic, social, or cultural needs of black students, she concludes. Wilkinson, a sociology professor at the University of Kentucky in Lexington, has written extensively on race and ethnic group relations.

As you read, consider the following questions:

1. According to one of the teachers Wilkinson cites, why do black students engage in "attention-seeking behavior"?
2. How has forced integration affected the experiences of black students in the 1990s, in the author's opinion?
3. In what ways were segregated schools healthier for black students, according to Wilkinson?

W̶ith the waning of the twentieth century, among the central questions that remain in the United States are those
involving interracial relations. Specifically: (1) Was the dismantling of the black segregated school a "necessary and sufficient"
condition for structural integration? (2) What have been the be-
havioral, psychological, academic, and cultural consequences of
[court-ordered school desegregation] on a heretofore ecologi-
cally isolated and economically powerless yet close-knit and
communal population? . . .

To illustrate the theme of this exploration into the cultural
and social psychological effects of forced public school integration on African American children, . . . the voices of two teachers of African descent will be introduced. This supporting information renders a profile of the contemporary integration crisis
and the myth of the benefits of racial association in the elementary, middle, and secondary grades.

The paradoxical character of racially based structural integration in the public school context is evident. This integration
dilemma emanates from a race-conscious society and a judicial
declaration regarding the constitutionality of dual systems and
the presumed negative impact of the all-black school. With respect to this, it is the thesis of this discussion that public school
integration and the associated demolition of the black school
has had a devastating impact on African American children—
their self-esteem, motivation to succeed, conceptions of heroes
or role models, respect for adults, and academic performance.
Racial animosities have also intensified. Unless rational alterna-
tives are devised that take into account the uniqueness of the
African American heritage, busing and compulsory school integration will become even more destructive to their health and
ultimately to the nation as a whole. . . .

SCHOOL INTEGRATION IS COUNTERPRODUCTIVE

To address the challenge of documenting and critically evaluating the impact of forced school integration on African American
children, I interviewed two of my first cousins who have taught
in public schools for more than twenty-five years. Products of
rigid discrimination and a segregated school system, both
women are competent and effective teachers. They have also experienced profound transformations in the social organization
of elementary and secondary schools. Their voices are representative of others across the country. The first, who has taught for
over thirty years, offers critical insights into the integration
quandary. When asked to describe how school desegregation has

affected African American children, she stated:

> The black child has gotten cheated through integration with lots of whites. [The] black child has to prove himself [or herself]. With integration, [we] got more money, better facilities, better textbooks. [But] what is missing is nurturing and the caring. This has had negative effects. Kids who could have been leaders are pretty much ignored. [You] can't ignore somebody and expect them to behave, to fit in.

She expressed deep concern about one practice that harms the learning potential of African American students: frequently and disproportionately issuing them hall passes. Such permissions are excuses to "get in the hall" and out of the classroom. Unfortunately, there is a tendency for teachers to approve hall passes "just to get rid of them." On the other hand, "to say 'no' indicates caring." She noted that since African American students often do not receive positive feedback in the classroom, those who congregate in the halls tend to be loud because "they're seeking negative attention." In the middle-class white environment, this attention-seeking behavior ultimately crystallizes animosity and racist stereotypes.

THE IRONY OF INTEGRATION

Another cousin, who has also taught for over twenty-five years in different grades as well as in special education, was asked: "What has integration done for or to African American children?" With wisdom and understanding of elementary and secondary school cultures, she observed irony in the fact that integration has actually "separated our black kids. It has divided them." Racial stratification and separation permeate the integrated school.

> The ones they bus to schools are from the projects. Integration prevents these kids from participating in extracurricular activities. They have to ride the bus and can't participate in clubs, organizations. As far as the parents are concerned, they are from the projects and don't have access to transportation.

> You get a few of these kids in one school; they group together. They want to be seen; they become behavior problems. Then, they're put in special education classes; [or] they're put in behavior disorder classes. They congregate. They don't do their work, [thus] they're labeled as slow. Then they're tracked. What happens as a result of that? Low self-esteem. "I'm slow anyway, so why try?"

> It's interesting that black kids are a minority in the [white] school but a majority in the special education and behavior disorder classes.

[At meal time,] they go by classes to the cafeteria. They go in and look for each other. They get together and become noisy. Then, they are put on school suspension.

I then asked if she thought this peculiar form of integration could work. Her immediate response was no. She stated that what has evolved is not interracial desegregation but racial exclusion.

I don't think it's integration. I think it's separation. The kids live in the projects across from each other. [However], in the morning, they're separated by busing. That's why when they get to school, they look for people like themselves.

Additionally, the social life of African American teenage girls has been affected severely by the breakup of the communal black high school. "They don't have any black guys to date. [But] black guys will date white girls." Thus, few African American youth participate in student activities. From this alienating social world, it is highly probable that the cycle of alienation experienced in the middle and high school years may be a prime factor in dropout rates, interracial tension, teenage pregnancy, and the number of female-headed households. . . .

The views of two talented teachers—who experienced segregation and the changing character of public schools—reveal the multiple human costs associated with displacing the black school and forcing children to integrate. Presently, children and adolescents in the United States, who live in familiar enclaves, are the victims of structurally based philosophies that have not taken into account the intergenerational fragmentation and psychological impairment of African American children's identities and hopes. Integration in elementary, middle, and high schools across the country is simply not working. Racial animosities are at an all-time high. African American children are not developing in constructive and unbiased environments. As many middle-class teachers enter the classroom with negative attitudes toward them and their parents, their feelings of self-worth and academic potential are damaged.

Where busing has been used to propel integration, when there are few black students in a classroom, they experience prolonged isolation in a predominantly white setting. Excluded from learning opportunities, they are also disengaged from student social circles that result in the cultivation of leadership skills and lasting friendships. Furthermore, minimal communication transpires between white teachers and African American parents. One disturbing result is that too often the Parent Teacher Association tends not to represent a cohesive and meaningful bond between the family and the neighborhood. Because parents lack an understanding of what occurs in the classroom, they feel a loss of control.

Essentially, in a historically race-conscious country founded on the ideology of white supremacy, separate facilities, amenities, and services in all institutional spheres will always be unequal. Even in a "desegregated" or partially integrated society, the economically deprived and politically disenfranchised will never be treated fairly. The destruction of the healthy aspects of African American family life that flowed from the sense of community under segregation will have a permanent influence on African Americans and the larger society. Although segregated schools were "separate and unequal," within their boundaries African American children were not exposed to denigrating racial imagery from the teachers, tracking, low expectations, or race hatred. Hence, the constitutional and structural benefits gained from obligatory school integration do not outweigh the immeasurable cultural and psychological losses. As Chicago attorney Thomas Hood stated at a meeting of the Kentucky African American Heritage Commission, "the same people in charge of desegregation had been in charge of segregation. Instead of integrating, they disintegrated." Such an occurrence epitomizes genuine "reverse discrimination."

"Desegregation . . . tends to produce better educational preparation and better chances for college and careers."

INTEGRATED EDUCATION FOSTERS EQUAL OPPORTUNITY

Gary Orfield

Gary Orfield is a professor at the Harvard Graduate School of Education and director of its Project on School Desegregation. In the following viewpoint, Orfield argues that public-school integration can help to alleviate the effects of societal discrimination on minority students. While some desegregation efforts have not been successful, the author maintains, well-planned desegregation programs at many middle-class suburban schools offer minority students high-quality educations and chances for future success. Orfield concludes that policymakers should not allow past failures to thwart present and future school-desegregation efforts.

As you read, consider the following questions:

1. In Orfield's opinion, what has caused America's "backward movement" toward segregation in schools?
2. According to the author, how did conservative opinion about the country's racial patterns affect school-desegregation efforts?
3. What was the purpose of the Emergency School Aid Act, according to Orfield?

From Gary Orfield, "America Lacks Equal Opportunity . . . and It Shows Acutely in Los Angeles," *Los Angeles Times*, December 28, 1993. Reprinted by permission of the author.

America's schools are slipping backward toward increased isolation of African American and Latino students by both race and poverty. Black students are losing some of the gains of the last 25 years and Latino students have become steadily more segregated over the same period.

This national backward movement is not the result of white flight to private schools; the proportion of whites who attended public schools in 1992 was actually higher than it was in 1972; their absolute numbers are down, however, because of a declining white birth rate. Instead, it is a result of government policies, the spread of residential segregation, the fragmentation of school districts in our metropolitan areas and the great increase in the numbers of minority students, particularly Latino students, in our country.

A MISGUIDED ANALYSIS

One of the most dramatic consequences of the conservative triumph of the 1970s and 1980s was the implicit assumption that nothing could be done about the nation's racial patterns. The conservative analysis held that government attempts were doomed to failure, and that, somehow, people in isolated minority communities would pull themselves up by their own bootstraps if only they were forced to do so. People were led to believe that vast amounts of taxpayer money were wasted on desegregation, and that we should try to upgrade neighborhood schools instead.

The truth is otherwise.

Americans of all racial and ethnic groups share a vision of college and middle-class success for their children, but only white children routinely go to schools that are middle class. Only 4% of white schools have a majority of poor children, compared with three-fifths of schools with more than 90% black and Latino students. These schools are far less likely to give students the credentials and connections necessary to function in middle-class settings.

Many people in big cities look at their overwhelmingly minority school enrollments and say that while desegregation might once have been a good idea, nothing can be done now. They are partially right. Under existing policies, it is unlikely that many of the students inside the district can be integrated with whites. Much can still be done, however, particularly in encouraging balance in suburban schools.

It's also wrong to see integration with whites as the only relevant standard. In San Francisco, the outstanding high school,

Lowell, has a large nonwhite majority, with Chinese students as the dominant group, but it represents a valuable opportunity for integration and educational gain for African American and Latino youths. We have to think about integration as a path into a much more broadly defined and multiethnic middle-class mainstream. Institutions of any sort that serve only the poor are unlikely to be highly effective. Multiracial middle-class schools, however, offer excellent preparation. The fact that a total solution is not possible is no excuse for doing nothing to alleviate obvious inequalities of schooling.

THE FAILINGS OF SEPARATE BUT EQUAL

Separate but equal may offer a salve to black pride and a comfort to white suburbanites; but there's not much proof that it works. In *The Closing Door*, Gary Orfield, a standard-bearer of white liberal integrationism, and co-author Carole Ashkinaze analyze the effects of the 1980 decision known as the Atlanta Compromise, in which that city's largely white power structure agreed to black control over the schools in exchange for an end to litigation that would have mandated desegregation throughout the metropolitan area. Here was separate but equal in laboratory form, presided over by a new black superintendent who had a national reputation as an educational reformer. Said former Atlanta mayor Andrew Young, "It was really the integration of the money to provide a quality education for all children that was black folks' goal. Racial balance was a means for achieving the goal." But despite an initial promise of success, Orfield concludes, "Huge numbers of children flunked grades and became more likely to drop out before completing high school," while "whites and middle-class blacks abandoned the city system in droves." Poor black students, in other words, were more isolated, and even more deeply cut off from the opportunity to develop, than they had been before.

James Traub, *Harper's Magazine*, June 1994.

In cities with well-designed programs, desegregation has been a success, even where busing was required. Metropolitan Louisville, Ky., has practiced city-suburban busing and instituted major educational reforms since 1975. A court order was lifted in 1980, but residents rejected proposals to quit using a smorgasbord of desegregation methods. Desegregation has not eliminated racial gaps, but it tends to produce better educational preparation and better chances for college and careers. In fact, what the Supreme Court found in 1954 is still true: Separate is unequal.

While we have spent vast amounts of money unsuccessfully

trying to upgrade segregated neighborhood schools, the only significant program that supported integration, the Emergency School Aid Act, was repealed in the early 1980s during the first Reagan Administration. This program did not coerce anyone and it did not pay for busing. It did pay for help in working out the education and human-relations problems of interracial schools and supporting innovations. ESAA had bipartisan support in Congress, was widely popular among urban school districts and produced positive evaluations of its benefits in human relations and educational achievement. It was madness to repeal this program in a fragile, multiracial society. It should be reinstated.

DESEGREGATION IS A VITAL STEP

Successful school desegregation programs can make a tremendous difference. Ultimately, of course, to provide a sound education for poor, minority children, we will have to address the broader issues of unemployment and isolation in strictly segregated, poverty-stricken communities. We must free our society from its greatest historical burden: the eviscerated promise of equal opportunity. We have lost sight of that goal in a generation of politicians exploiting racial fears on a national level.

We are still blessed with reasonably strong institutions and a set of dreams shared across racial and ethnic lines. It is very important that there be a real possibility of this vision coming true for all children if our society is to be viable. Integrated schools are not the whole answer, but they are a vital step.

> "A [multiracial] category . . . would
> have no value in terms of civil rights
> enforcement."

A MULTIRACIAL CATEGORY WOULD LEAD TO INCREASED DISCRIMINATION

Raul Yzaguirre

The U.S. Census Bureau's standard racial classifications provide information used to enforce civil rights policies. Some policy analysts, however, advocate the addition of a multiracial category as a more accurate classification for people of mixed racial heritage. In the following viewpoint, Raul Yzaguirre contends that a multiracial census category would endanger equal opportunity for Hispanic Americans. Because the proposed category is not clearly defined, he asserts, many Latinos would classify themselves as multiracial rather than Hispanic. Such confusion, Yzaguirre argues, would cause undercounting of Hispanic populations, which in turn could allow the development of public policy that ignores discrimination against Latinos. Yzaguirre is the president of the National Council of La Raza, an organization that seeks to improve opportunities for Hispanic Americans.

As you read, consider the following questions:

1. Why do many Hispanics identify themselves as white, black, Asian, or American Indian, according to Yzaguirre?
2. According to the author, what is the major purpose of collecting data on race?
3. Why would a multiracial census category lead to inaccurate data collection, in Yzaguirre's opinion?

From Raul Yzaguirre, "Multiracial Category Would Make Many Hispanics Invisible," *San Diego North County Times,* July 21, 1996. Reprinted by permission of the author.

The question for Latinos is whether we count as Americans. The Census Bureau may be undermining our efforts to be treated as equal citizens under the law.

Since 1977, the Office of Management and Budget has required the Census Bureau to use standard classifications in collecting and reporting data on racial and ethnic groups. As the major official source of detailed information on the U.S. population, census data are crucial to the formulation of public policy. Clear and consistent federal data collection on race and ethnic groups has gone a long way in ensuring civil rights, due-process protections and equal allocation of federal resources to minority groups and economically disadvantaged communities.

From the perspective of the U.S. Latino community, known as Hispanics to the Census Bureau, accurate collection and reporting of these data is critical. Many civil rights laws rely on race and ethnic data to ensure effective enforcement in such key areas as education, voting, employment and housing.

This data gathering is now imperiled by a new "multiracial" category. Its proponents argue that existing identifiers are too rigid. They suggest that, as the population of Americans with mixed racial background grows, the existing categories do not and cannot accommodate people who identify with all elements of their heritage.

Some of these arguments resonate with Latinos, a multiracial population with origins in Latin American, European and African countries. Hispanics comprise an ethnic group whose identity crosses racial boundaries, so they often identify themselves as white, black, Asian or American Indian. It is this racial and cultural diversity that is the very essence of American culture.

THE IMPORTANCE OF CENSUS DATA

The current categories permit us to compare the status of major subgroups, such as Puerto Ricans, Cuban Americans, Mexican Americans and Central Americans.

But census classifications are not designed to illuminate every group's sense of cultural diversity, nor are they a forum for expression of every person's distinct, individual identity.

Instead, the major purpose of collecting race and ethnic data is to profile the economic and social status of groups of people who have something in common.

For example, census data tell us that irrespective of subgroup, Hispanics experience disproportionate levels of discrimination, poverty, undereducation and unemployment.

As currently proposed, a multiracial category would include

any person of mixed ancestry. Of those who identify as multiracial, some may have black and white parents, and some may have Asian American and American Indian parents. Such a category would have little practical use for the purpose of assessing the socioeconomic status of recognized groups, and would have no value in terms of civil rights enforcement.

THE PROPOSED CATEGORY IS CONFUSING

A multiracial category would lead to vast confusion and inaccurate data collection. Test surveys reveal that many respondents are confused by the new category, and respond in inappropriate ways. Because the very definition of "multiracial" is itself unclear, even respondents who are not multiracial may identify themselves as such. Some white respondents in test surveys have marked "multiracial" while selecting a mix of ethnic identifiers like German-white.

This confusion is particularly dangerous for Hispanics. According to the General Accounting Office, 98 percent of respondents who classified themselves as "other race" in the 1990 census were Hispanic. On the census form, the questions related to ethnicity are placed after the questions related to race. Because of this placement, Census Bureau research has shown that Latinos already are the most undercounted group in the United States. If a multiracial question were added, many Latinos might select "multiracial" as their identifier, and never get to the Hispanic question.

OPPOSITION TO THE MULTIRACIAL CATEGORY

Those who oppose a multiracial category believe the current system is flawed enough. Trying to refine it, they say, would give it more credibility than it deserves. Candy Mills, founding editor of Atlanta-based magazines *Interrace* and *Child of Colors*, which are aimed at the multiracial market, believes society should be moving toward eliminating all categories rather than adding to them.

"It has no meaning. It doesn't mean that all multiracial people have any shared experience. All it does is validate all the other racial categories as pure," she says.

Gary Younge, *Washington Post National Weekly Edition*, July 24–August 4, 1996.

The existing categories are not perfect. For instance, I am the product of European and American Indian ancestors. My children respect equally my Hispanic heritage and my wife's European heritage. We are a multiracial, multiethnic family, but we do not subscribe to a single multiracial identity. For us, the existing system does capture our shared identity, however imperfectly. We are all Hispanics, who may be of any race.

While a new multiracial category may appear attractive on the surface, the addition of an ambiguous and confusing identifier does more harm than good.

The new multiracial category would have the unintended effect of increasing the undercounting of the Hispanic population and concentrating a number of Latinos into a new, ambiguous classification, thus rendering them invisible.

> "Even though the government tries mightily to define who belongs in which racial category, its racial definitions make no sense."

A MULTIRACIAL CATEGORY WOULD NOT LEAD TO INCREASED DISCRIMINATION

Judy Scales-Trent

Some civil rights observers believe that adding a new multiracial category to U.S. census surveys will result in discrimination against minorities whose populations would therefore be under-counted. In the following viewpoint, Judy Scales-Trent disagrees with this argument. Although she questions the entire concept of government-created racial categories, she contends that the ethnic population count in itself does not prevent discrimination because the government can choose to ignore such statistics when deciding on civil rights policies. Scales-Trent is a law professor at the State University of New York in Buffalo and the author of *Notes of a White Black Woman: Race, Color, Community*.

As you read, consider the following questions:

1. According to Scales-Trent, how has the U.S. census created and re-created racial categories?
2. In the author's opinion, what is strange about questions concerning "pure" or "mixed" racial descent?
3. In Scales-Trent's opinion, what issue lies under the census controversy?

From Judy Scales-Trent, "Add 'Multiracial' to the Next Census," *Los Angeles Times*, July 3, 1996. Reprinted by permission of the author.

In preparation for the census in the year 2000, the government is holding hearings around the country on the issue of whether it should revise its current racial categories—black, white, Asian/Pacific Islander and American Indian.

The government has been creating racial categories and classifying citizens by race during the census for at least a hundred years. And every 10 years it changes its mind about what those various "races" might be. For example, in 1890, there were four separate categories of African Americans. Between 1950 and 1970, Asian Indians were considered "white." Mexican Americans, too, used to be counted as "white"; today, they are in the census' only ethnic category, "Hispanic origin," which can be any race.

These formal changes remind us that "race" is created, then re-created over time. Now there is a move underway for allowing "multiracial" as an answer to "What is your race?" Some of those who want the "multiracial" category joined a march on Washington on July 20, 1996, to support this change. March organizer Charles Michael Byrd said that adding this category would be a "step toward doing away with the whole concept of race."

This option is favored by many people who have, for example, one parent who is white and one who is black. For them it is a powerful issue of family identity. But many civil rights groups oppose this option for fear that the count of, say, black Americans will be diminished if the choice "multiracial" appears. They argue that statistical data about black Americans has been helpful for civil rights gains.

AN INFORMATIVE DEBATE

In my view, the debate is helpful for the whole country because it highlights our confusion about race and our bigotry.

I am a civil rights lawyer who has been practicing, teaching and writing about civil rights law for 25 years. Most recently, I have used my vantage point as a black American with white skin to write about how Americans create race on an ongoing basis. And I have come to the conclusion that the question of "mixed" ("multiracial") and "pure" racial groups is bizarre, because, even though the government tries mightily to define who belongs in which racial category, its racial definitions make no sense. For example, the current rule states that you are black if you "have origins in any of the black racial groups of Africa"; you are white if you "have origins in any of the original [sic] white groups of Europe." Now, tell me: Who among us knows their "origins"? For if you count back in your own family, doubling the number each generation (two parents, four grandparents, eight great-grandparents, etc.) you will find 32,000 possible ancestors during the previous 15 generations alone. Do you know their "origins"? What could "pure" or "mixed" possibly mean in that context?

THE NEED FOR A MULTIRACIAL CATEGORY

The least the Census Bureau should do is add a "multiracial" category to the census choices to reflect the rapidly increasing number of people of mixed-race heritage, the offspring of 'biracial' or multiracial parents. Interracial marriages have been increasing rapidly in recent years, especially between blacks and whites. The 1990 census counted 3 million people who said they were married to or living with a person of another race. They had about 2 million biracial or multiracial children.

Americans of other minorities intermarry in much larger percentages, up to 12 percent for Asian men, 25 percent for Asian women and 60 percent for American Indians. Their children do not fit comfortably or honestly into the racial categories used not only by the Census Bureau but by the federal government as a whole.

Joan Beck, *San Diego North County Times*, July 21, 1996.

Rep. Tom Sawyer (D-Ohio), who chaired the House subcommittee that held hearings on this issue, put it this way: "We seem to have this sense of this illusion of purity, that on the one hand we act as though we know what we are talking about when we refer to notions such as race and ethnicity. I am not sure we have even the vaguest idea."

THE PROPOSED CATEGORY RAISES IMPORTANT QUESTIONS

I disagree, however, with the notion that adding a "multiracial" category will be a "step toward doing away with the concept of race." Let's not forget that Nazi Germany created a special racial category for the children of Aryans and Jews (Mischlinge), and that South Africa created the category "coloured" for those people it considered "mixed." These were not progressive acts. They were the acts of oppressive regimes trying to rationalize their oppression.

I also disagree with those who argue that adding the category would make civil rights gains more unlikely by reducing the count of, say, black Americans. Statistical data can help improve the lot of black Americans—but only when white Americans want this to happen; the numbers themselves have no independent power. For example, Congress can ignore—and has ignored—powerful statistics about the plight of black Americans when it sets its legislative agenda. Similarly, in cases where there is strong statistical proof of discrimination, the Supreme Court can change—and has changed—how it interprets civil rights law in order to minimize the power of those statistics.

The question of whether there should be a "multiracial" category brings these issues to the fore. But don't think that changing census categories will necessarily change lives. The only way to improve the lives of black Americans is to address the issue that lies under the census controversy: why this country has always worked so aggressively to sort its people by race. It is clear that America creates race, then sorts by race, in order to create a hierarchy—in order to determine who is supposed to win and who is supposed to lose. As long as we refuse to address this underlying dynamic, the lives of those whom America puts at the bottom will remain desperately hard.

PERIODICAL BIBLIOGRAPHY

The following articles have been selected to supplement the diverse views presented in this chapter. Addresses are provided for periodicals not indexed in the *Readers' Guide to Periodical Literature*, the *Alternative Press Index*, the *Social Sciences Index*, or the *Index to Legal Periodicals and Books*.

Douglas A. Blackmon	"The Resegregation of a Southern School," *Harper's Magazine*, September 1992.
Valerie Burgher	"Silent Racism," *Nation*, April 17, 1995.
Dinesh D'Souza	"Is Racism a Western Idea?" *American Scholar*, Autumn 1995.
Eric Foner	"The Great Divide," *Nation*, October 30, 1995.
George M. Fredrickson	"Demonizing the American Dilemma," *New York Review of Books*, Oct 19, 1995.
Randall Kennedy	"Is All Discrimination Created Equal?" *Time*, October 16, 1995.
James S. Kunen	"The End of Integration," *Time*, April 29, 1996.
Jon Nordheimer	"Police Accused of Searches Based on Race," *New York Times*, December 23, 1994.
Orlando Patterson	"The Paradox of Integration," *New Republic*, November 6, 1995.
Ray C. Rist	"Color, Class, and the Realities of Inequality," *Society*, March/April 1996.
James Traub	"Can Separate Be Equal?" *Harper's Magazine*, June 1994.
U.S. News & World Report	"Race on Campus," April 19, 1993.
Jack E. White	"Growing Up in Black and White," *Time*, May 17, 1993.
Robert L. Woodson	"The End of Racism? Hardly," *New York Times*, September 23, 1995.
Wendy Murray Zoba	"Separate and Equal," *Christianity Today*, February 5, 1996.

CHAPTER 3

ARE CLAIMS OF REVERSE DISCRIMINATION VALID?

CHAPTER PREFACE

In February 1994, the Los Angeles Fire Department prohibited five thousand white applicants from taking its job examination. According to writer and lecturer Allan C. Brownfeld, "This injustice resulted from a 1974 consent decree between the city of Los Angeles and the Justice Department [requiring] the fire department to hire fifty percent of its firefighters from among minority groups." To ensure that the correct amount of minorities would be hired, he maintains, the department barred a certain number of whites from taking the preliminary test.

Many Americans believe that this and other affirmative action policies and quotas actually discriminate against whites, particularly white men. Such "reverse discrimination," critics argue, pervades American society and endangers equal opportunity for white males. As Mike Callahan, a white Chicago firefighter, explained to the *Washington Post*, racial-preference policies "are creating a new class of the downtrodden and that's us."

However, other workers and policymakers contend that reverse discrimination does not exist. Commentator Theodore William Allen argues that critics of affirmative action ignore America's continuing history of preferential hiring due to family ties, school connections, "old boy" friendship networks, and veteran status. While preferential hiring of whites is still widely accepted and practiced, Allen maintains, preferential hiring of qualified women and minorities to make up for past discrimination is unfairly criticized.

Furthermore, asserts ethnic studies professor June Jordan, women and people of color are being unjustly blamed for the shrinking opportunities in the U.S. workforce. In Jordan's opinion, many companies feel threatened by an unstable economy and are therefore hiring fewer workers. This economic instability, she points out, has led to a reduction in job security for all Americans. At the same time, she maintains, women and people of color have made some gains in the workforce because of affirmative action. Jordan argues that these minority gains have been wrongly perceived as losses for white males in the labor force.

Claims of reverse discrimination in the workforce and on the college campus are the subject of intense debate. The viewpoints in the following chapter explore this controversy.

"Race and gender quotas . . . have devastated the lives and careers of countless people with limited legal resources to fight back."

AFFIRMATIVE ACTION CREATES REVERSE DISCRIMINATION

Steven Yates

Affirmative action policies are intended to ensure equal opportunity for minorities and women. However, Steven Yates argues in the following viewpoint, affirmative action policies create quotas by requiring that a certain number of job positions be filled by minorities or women. According to Yates, these quotas force employers to hire a predetermined number of minorities and women, thereby discriminating against qualified white males. Even when white employers hire a number of minorities, he contends, they can still face damaging lawsuits if they have not followed all of the strict quota guidelines. Yates is the author of *Civil Wrongs: What Went Wrong with Affirmative Action*, from which this viewpoint is excerpted.

As you read, consider the following questions:

1. How do affirmative action policies harm minorities, according to the author?
2. How does Yates define "covert discrimination"?
3. According to to Yates, why did the Equal Employment Opportunity Commission charge Mike Welbel with racial discrimination?

A ffirmative action and related policies have been a source of growing discontent and division in our society since the 1970s. Arrayed on one side of the debate are those who begin by observing that this country's past treatment of its racial and ethnic minorities and of women is a blight on its history. Advocates of this position maintain that justice requires some kind of systematic policy aimed at remedying the effects of long-standing discrimination against blacks, other minorities, and women. . . .

[In addition], say affirmative action advocates, full repair of the damage done in the past requires that women and members of minority groups have equal employment opportunities in the present and future. The Civil Rights Act of 1964 and Voting Rights Act of 1965 did not eradicate patterns of discrimination that still concentrate power and influence in the hands of white men of European descent. Thus a long period of sustained government action is needed to counteract these patterns by mandating and enforcing affirmative action.

THE CRITICS OF AFFIRMATIVE ACTION

On the other side are those who contend that affirmative action has replaced discrimination against women and minorities with discrimination against white men—reverse discrimination. Critics of affirmative action argue that while such ideals as equal employment opportunity sound good in principle, in practice they have come to conceal equally unjust, equally harmful, and probably unconstitutional practices that give preference to some at the expense of others.

These practices, critics add, have replaced individual rights with group entitlements, and the concept of equal opportunity with demands for equal outcomes, which in turn have produced quotas in workplace hiring and promoting, in government subcontracting, and in college admissions and faculty hiring. The result has been compromised standards throughout the economy and the educational system. These policies have undermined the long-standing ideal of admitting students to college, hiring and promoting employees, and awarding contracts on the basis of merit rather than politics.

By creating a climate of dependence—which actually penalizes efforts by individual members of minorities to succeed on their own merits—affirmative action has reinforced the worst stereotypes of members of "protected groups" as consisting of people unable to "make it on their own." Preferential policies have added fuel to racial tensions by incurring the resentment of those not in protected groups, those who are expected to pay the costs of reparation despite never having engaged in discriminatory practices themselves. . . .

THE TERMS OF THE DEBATE

Backers of affirmative action nonetheless contend that terms like "reverse discrimination" and "quotas" are red herrings concocted by white men who fear losing their long-established privileges. To the extent preferential treatment does occur, they maintain, it is justified by the fact that because of past discrimination most women and minorities are too far behind economically to compete effectively. The claim that they can be expected to "play catch up" by their own efforts alone is said to be naive, since it ignores long-standing patterns of discrimination that remain prevalent despite decades of counter-efforts. As for the objection that affirmative action "lowers standards," have these standards not always been set by white men? As for hiring on the basis of merit, does anyone really believe we have ever had a genuine meritocracy in this country?

© Mike Ramirez. Reprinted by permission of Copley News Service.

These two camps have been at loggerheads now since the 1970s, and many have despaired of ever reaching a rational resolution. Reasonable people can and do disagree, particularly when their disagreements stem from fundamentally different moral and philosophical convictions. And it has not always been clear what principles we should appeal to when attempting to resolve disputes such as this. But some opinions are nevertheless superior to others, since they are better supported with reasons and available evidence. This is my most basic assumption—indeed, without it further inquiry would be pointless.

Misguided Racial Policies

I have found that there are good reasons why the critics of affirmative action and kindred policies now have the better of the argument. As we look past the arguments presented by the believers to the realities of implementation, the picture that emerges shows the critics to be essentially correct. Thus continued efforts to implement race-conscious policies by force should be disturbing to every American—of whatever racial or ethnic background—who wants to live in a free society.

To use the term "quotas" raises the hackles of affirmative action advocates, who claim that quotas are figments of right-wing imagination. Talk of quotas, they say, merely plays to our worst racial fears and hostilities. However, we can cut through at least some of the semantics by considering the existence of quotas as a question that can be investigated empirically like any other empirical question.

Quotas Are Real

I have concluded that quotas do exist. They are real and have devastated the lives and careers of many people without significantly helping those in targeted groups. The Supreme Court decision *Griggs* (1971) seems to have completed the transformation of civil rights legislation from mandating nondiscrimination to mandating preferences. Before *Griggs*, discrimination meant "an action taken by some individual or organization of individuals against another individual, e.g., refusal to hire for a desirable position, based on a group characteristic." After *Griggs*, it came to mean simply "lack of a politically acceptable statistical percentage." (What determined "political acceptability" was usually the percentage of members of targeted groups in the local or regional population.)

Thus we came to hear expressions such as "covert discrimination," which could be traced to no actions on the part of anyone but which nonetheless was assumed to be responsible for any statistical disparity between groups. Attempting to rectify covert discrimination by legislative and judicial force throughout institution after institution has produced what sociologist Frederick R. Lynch compared to a steamroller, flattening everything in its path. . . .

Consider the strange case of *Equal Employment Opportunity Commission v. The Daniel Lamp Co.*, featured on the March 24, 1991, segment of the CBS television news program *60 Minutes*. Daniel Lamp is a small company located in a poor, mostly Hispanic area in southeastern Chicago. It manufactures lamps from used parts and then sells them to furniture stores around the city. Owner Mike Welbel is a self-made entrepreneur, a one-time traveling salesman who had borrowed $3,000 on a Chevy station wagon and started his own business nine years earlier. Welbel is white; his workforce, which varies in size from under twelve to over thirty employees, has always been nearly all Hispanic and black. This did not prevent the Equal Employment Opportunity Commission (EEOC) from accusing him of racial discrimination and filing suit based on an allegation made by a black woman who applied for a job with the company in early 1989 and was not hired. As Welbel tells it, one day EEOC representatives showed up at his office and demanded to see his employment records. He cooperated fully, believing he had nothing to hide. The EEOC then demanded that Welbel pay not only $340.01 to the woman who was not hired, but also $123,991 to six other blacks who allegedly applied for jobs at Daniel Lamp during 1988 and 1989 but weren't hired. In addition, Welbel was ordered to buy newspaper advertisements at the cost of around $10,000 of his own money to locate these individuals!

COVERT DISCRIMINATION?

Welbel's description of his initial reaction as told to Morley Safer of *60 Minutes* is worth repeating:

> I froze. I froze in my chair. I—I—I was—I was—I—I got—I started feeling my chest bouncing around. I don't—I don't think it was a heart attack, but I'll tell you something. It was the next thing to it. I just was frozen with shock.

The following exchange between Safer and Jim Lafferty, director of legislative affairs at the EEOC, occurred during the program:

> *Safer* (interviewing): . . . quite apart from records, doesn't your nose tell you that this really isn't much of a case and that Mike Welbel is probably not a racist? He's a little guy trying to . . . make a living . . .

> *Lafferty:* Well, unfortunately, we have to rely on, not only the statistics, but on the word of Lucille Johnson and seven other people who've come forward since then telling us that they had also experienced discrimination during that period at Daniel Lamp.

Safer (voiceover): What helped to make Lafferty's case against Mike Welbel was the EEOC's computer. It told the agency that, based on 363 companies employing 100 or more people and located within a three-mile radius of Daniel Lamp, Daniel Lamp should employ at any given moment exactly 8.45 blacks, which to Mike Welbel sounded like a quota. And the law says the EEOC can't set quotas.

Lafferty: We really haven't said that. What we've said is, "These are what the companies around you are doing. You've discriminated against this—"

Safer: Stop being a federal bureaucrat for a minute and tell me what you're really telling him. What are you really telling him?

Lafferty: Don't discriminate. Obey the law.

Safer: But if he has three black employees and doesn't hire a fourth for whatever reason and that fourth accused him of discrimination, do you prosecute?

Lafferty: Yes, we do. It's not that there's a magic number. Please believe me. We don't set magical numbers for people like Mr. Welbel to meet.

Safer (voiceover): That's what Mr. Lafferty says, but, in a sense, it did set numbers by telling Mike that, based on other larger companies' personnel, Daniel Lamp should employ 8.45 blacks.

Welbel: Any way you slice the pie, it's a quota system.

Safer: But if they say, "Look, Mike, you've got to have eight blacks working for you," could you live with that?

Welbel: Could I live with it? Yes. Is it more difficult than hiring by qualification? Yes. What the government is asking me to do is hire by color. They're saying, "Look, this black individual may not be as qualified, but that's who we want to see in your workplace." What they've become is—They do the hiring and I run the place under their direction. I no longer decide who's good and who's bad.

Daniel Lamp eventually reached a settlement with the EEOC. This was fortunate, for had the lawsuit gone to court and Welbel lost, he would have been out of business and his minority employees would have been out on the street—put there by the very organization that purports to represent their interests. The details of the settlement have been kept secret but, needless to say, Welbel now employs a numerically correct number of blacks at Daniel Lamp.

The struggle to eliminate racial quotas from our legal system has so far failed. Defenders of [affirmative action legislation] continue to maintain that this legislation does not create quotas and that complaints about quotas are inherently racist. The exact opposite is the case. Race and gender quotas have existed in American society ever since the Nixon administration. They have devastated the lives and careers of countless people with limited legal resources to fight back.

| "Affirmative action is not the source
of discrimination, but the vehicle
for removing the effects of
discrimination."

AFFIRMATIVE ACTION DOES NOT CREATE REVERSE DISCRIMINATION

Nancy Stein et al.

The following viewpoint was prepared by a team coordinated by Nancy Stein, editor of the progressive journal *CrossRoads* and a member of the editorial board of *Social Justice*, a quarterly educational journal. The team consisted of Elizabeth Martinez, a *CrossRoads* editor; Cathy Tashiro, a doctoral student in sociology; and Phil Hutchings, program director of the Center for Ethics and Economic Policy in Berkeley, California. The authors assert that affirmative action is needed to ensure equal opportunity for people of color and women. Affirmative action does not impose quotas, they argue, nor does it require employers to hire unqualified minority applicants or to discriminate against white men. In the authors' opinion, many white workers blame affirmative action policies for a lack of jobs that is actually caused by a poor economic environment.

As you read, consider the following questions:

1. According to the authors, what do most employers use "merit" to justify?
2. In the authors' opinion, what is the difference between affirmative action policies and court-mandated quotas?
3. How do American institutions benefit from affirmative action, according to the authors?

From Nancy Stein et al., "Questions and Answers About Affirmative Action," *Social Justice*, Fall 1995. Reprinted by permission of *Social Justice*.

M any of the gains won by the civil rights movements of the
1960s are now in danger of being overturned and affirmative action is rapidly becoming the most prominent target. . . . A
drumbeat of objections to affirmative action, loaded with misin-
formation and distortions, fills the mainstream media. We hope
the "Questions and Answers" presented here can help to correct
misconceptions and shed light on the reality of affirmative action
policies and their value for promoting equal opportunity for all.

LEVELING THE PLAYING FIELD

What is affirmative action?

Affirmative action is a policy to encourage equal opportunity
and to level the playing field for groups of people who have
been and are discriminated against. According to the Equal Employment Opportunity Commission, affirmative action "is considered essential to assuring that jobs are genuinely and equally
accessible to qualified persons, without regard to their sex,
racial, or ethnic characteristics."

The roots of affirmative action lie in the Civil Rights Act of
1964. At first, affirmative action aimed to eliminate racial imbal-
ance in hiring policies; later the goals were extended to include
college admissions and the awarding of government contracts.
Subsequent provisions extended protections to all people of
color, women, older people, and people with disabilities. Equal
opportunity laws ban discrimination. Affirmative action goes
farther by requiring employers to take "affirmative" steps to
achieve a balanced representation of workers.

A 1995 poll found that when questions are worded in clear
language about the implications of doing away with affirmative
action programs, 71% of whites believe that such programs
make "opportunities for everyone, including women and minorities" and 68% of those sampled approved the use of these
programs to achieve equal opportunity for all.

HIRING QUALIFIED PEOPLE

*Does affirmative action mean hiring or promoting unqualified people just because
they are minorities or women?*

No. First of all, affirmative action calls for the hiring of qualified people. Opponents of affirmative action say that to get qualified people, hiring policies should be based only on "merit," as
if other factors are not normally considered. There have always
been preferences, yet no one ever said they "lowered quality"
until they began to be applied for the benefit of people of color
and women.

Employers tend to hire people like themselves and to think of them as the most qualified. "Merit" becomes the justification for this. It is more difficult to see and trust the qualifications of someone who is different. Even a former Republican California State Senator doubted that "there are enough white employers who would hire people from minority communities without the encouragement of affirmative action policies."

Most jobs are found by word of mouth. Since neighborhoods and social networks tend to be segregated, word of mouth leads to the perpetuation of discrimination, intentionally or not. Affirmative action pushes employers to try harder, to cast a wider net. Without this extra effort, many employers would do what they have always done: maintain that they couldn't find a "qualified" woman or person of color and hire the white man they wanted anyway.

AN OVERSIMPLIFIED CONCEPT OF MERIT

The anti–affirmative action position assumes a narrow, oversimplified conception of merit based on test scores, grade-point average, or other measurable standards. Yet many tests are inadequate for predicting success. Numerous studies have found that there is only a slight relationship between test scores and performance or professional achievement. On the other hand, there is a major relationship between race, income level, educational resources, and test scores. Over-reliance on test results inhibits employers from considering other factors that indicate competence and predict success, such as prior work experience and specialized training. Regarding college admissions, tests are culturally biased in that they tend to reflect the experiences of middle-class students and their access to higher-quality education than that available to less-advantaged students.

Students are also frequently admitted on the basis of many preferences that have nothing to do with affirmative action, such as personal connections, financial contributions, geographical diversity, athletic skill, or whether an applicant is a veteran. "Far more whites have entered the gates of the 10 most elite institutions through 'alumni preference' than the combined numbers of all the Blacks and Chicanos entering through affirmative action," according to the *San Francisco Examiner*. Furthermore, children of alumni admitted to Harvard had SAT scores that averaged 35 points lower than other Harvard students.

The University of California sets aside a mere five percent of its incoming freshman class for those who do not meet certain standards, but who are members of an underrepresented racial group, athletes, or graduates of rural high schools, for example. The University of Washington School of Law receives 2,500 applications. About 900 are considered clearly qualified, but most are not accepted because there are only 165 first-year places. The law school selects students based on a combination of scores, grades, and other factors, such as cultural background and special talents to enhance the richness of the student body. There is no evidence that affirmative action has lowered the quality of any educational institution.

Does affirmative action mean quotas?

No. In 1976, Allan Bakke sued the University of California Medical School at Davis for denying him admission on the basis of reverse discrimination, because 16 out of 100 places in the medical school class were reserved for "economically and educationally disadvantaged applicants." The Supreme Court ruled in favor of Bakke, holding that the policy of reserving specified slots was a quota system and illegal. However, the Court also held that race could be included as a factor in determining admission, as long as it was not the exclusive basis on which a decision was made.

Affirmative action plans do not impose quotas; they simply seek to increase the pool of qualified applicants by using aggressive recruitment and outreach programs, setting goals and timetables, and establishing training programs, among other measures. People confuse affirmative action with "consent decrees," which are court-mandated quotas imposed by judges on specific institutions after years, often decades, of proven failure to end discrimination. Ending affirmative action would not affect consent decrees.

REMOVING THE EFFECTS OF DISCRIMINATION

Isn't affirmative action really reverse discrimination?

No. Affirmative action policies provide equal opportunity to those groups who have been systematically denied it. Affirmative action is not the source of discrimination, but the vehicle for removing the effects of discrimination. Some white men are opposed to giving others the opportunity they have historically enjoyed and so cry "reverse discrimination" in response to the steps that have been taken in that direction.

Actually, few reverse discrimination cases have been brought by white males and even fewer have been found to have any merit. A Labor Department report found fewer than 100 reverse discrimination cases among more than 3,000 discrimination opinions by the U.S. District Court and the Court of Appeals, between 1990 and 1994. Discrimination was established in only six cases. The report found that "many of the cases were the result of a disappointed applicant . . . erroneously assuming that when a woman or minority got the job, it was because of race or sex, not qualifications."

While some white men may feel they have been unfairly passed over, it is a myth that they are losing jobs to unqualified women and people of color due to affirmative action. While white men continue to dominate the upper levels of business, less-skilled white men, men of color, and women are all losing jobs as corporations move overseas, downsize, hire part-time workers, automate, and computerize. White workers are directing their anger at people of color and women, rather than at the corporate decisions that lead to increased economic insecurity for everyone. . . .

AFFIRMATIVE ACTION IS DEMOCRATIC

When conservatives complain that affirmative action is "reverse discrimination," it is largely an ideological ploy; they don't extend their indictment to government programs that privilege and thereby foster mobility for assorted businesses, veterans, and farmers, among others. In any event, job market breakthroughs for African-Americans in the last three decades have hardly diminished job opportunities for white males.

It is perfectly legitimate for a democracy to employ compensatory or reparational public policies to correct massive, long-standing, and cruel injuries that have been done to citizens. It was to the credit of the Kennedy and Johnson administrations (and bipartisan Republican supporters) in the 1960s that they decided to face the issue squarely and forge affirmative action. And it is crucial that affirmative action, with the strong support of the mainstream African-American leadership (the civil rights community), was democratized by its extension to women and Hispanics.

Martin Kilson, *Dissent*, Fall 1995.

Doesn't affirmative action stigmatize people of color who are seen as getting a job or into college only because of that policy?

Stereotypes plague people of color and would continue to do so even if this policy were eliminated. White people, however, have received preferential treatment for hundreds of years without being stigmatized for it. They held the exclusive right to most jobs without having to compete with anyone else. Now people of color are stigmatized by being told, "the only reason you're here is because of affirmative action." So they are faced with the constant need to prove that they are qualified.

Sometimes this makes people of color feel as though they would be better off without affirmative action programs so that it would be clear they "deserve" to be where they are. However, affirmative action was developed in the first place because many white people refused to recognize people of color as deserving an equal chance to demonstrate their abilities.

Why don't we change affirmative action to policies that help people based on economic need instead of race or gender?

This approach would benefit people of color who are disadvantaged economically. But counterpoising it to affirmative action is an attempt to sweep the pivotal issue of race under the rug. People of color have been discriminated against based entirely on race for hundreds of years. Therefore, policies to eliminate discrimination must address the issue of race. We need programs based on economic need in addition to, but not instead of, affirmative action.

A CHANGING ECONOMY

What is behind the attack on affirmative action?

First, the economy continues to decline. People are afraid of losing what they have. There is a scarcity of jobs and limited resources today. It was easier for society to accept the changes brought about by the civil rights and women's movements when the economy was growing and the middle class was still expanding. The current economy is seeing a shift from high-wage manufacturing jobs to low-wage service jobs, with a drop in the standard of living for middle-income workers, the decline of blue-collar unions, and lack of investment in public infrastructure.

Safety-net programs are also being cut deeply. The commitment to provide for people in need is fast disappearing. Women on welfare, teen mothers, immigrants, criminals, youth, and now anyone who benefits from affirmative action programs are depicted as undeserving and taking away from what others have.

This attack is taking place in the larger context of the fight for the identity of the nation. It is no accident that California is the first big site of battle. California will soon become the first state (other than Hawaii) to be majority non-white; the cities of Los Angeles, San Francisco, and some counties already are. Many people from the dominant society fear losing control over the economic, political, and cultural direction of the state, particularly to people from unfamiliar cultures. This converges with the economic problems and leads to the scapegoating of immigrants and other people of color, who are blamed for this crisis. While California and the nation need the labor of immigrants and other people of color, they do not wish to make room for them as human beings, let alone as equal participants in civic life.

Rolling back affirmative action fits in with the Republican agenda to limit the role of government in defending the vulnerable: deregulation, ending welfare, and cutting school lunch programs, food stamps, and other programs that benefit the poor. Underlying this attack is an aversion to the fundamental concept of an egalitarian society and an acceptance of living in a society polarized by race and gender.

THE NEED FOR AFFIRMATIVE ACTION

Does affirmative action benefit society as a whole?

Yes. Having a truly democratic and just society demands it because racism, sexism, and all discrimination tear at the very fabric of society. According to history professor Roger Wilkins, a nation that seeks to maintain privilege "abandons its soul . . . because so many people are excluded from the possibility of decent lives and from forming any sense of community with the rest of society."

Higher education has also benefitted from affirmative action. The President of the University of California, Jack Peltason, stated: "Equal opportunity, affirmative action, and diversity programs have been indispensable both to our educational mission and to our ability to achieve a diversified community of learning." Private corporations have embraced affirmative action, knowing that it is good business to have a work force that reflects the demographics of the community.

Elizabeth Toledo, coordinator for California NOW [National Organization for Women], believes that "We have to change the question from 'Is affirmative action good or bad?' to the question 'Does the government have the responsibility to address discrimination and bias in the workplace, and does it have a duty to attempt to create a level playing field?'"

The Dean of the University of Washington's Law School summed up why it does: "In an increasingly multicultural nation with a global reach, a commitment to diversity—to broadening the boundaries of inclusiveness of American institutions—is economically necessary, morally imperative, and constitutionally legitimate."

| "White males are now second class
| citizens under the law."

WHITE MEN FACE REVERSE DISCRIMINATION

Paul Craig Roberts

Paul Craig Roberts is a nationally syndicated columnist and a Distinguished Fellow at the Cato Institute, a libertarian public policy research organization in Washington, D.C. In the following viewpoint, Roberts argues that white males have become victims of reverse discrimination. He maintains that white men are hindered by negative stereotypes and affirmative action policies that grant preferential treatment to women and minorities. Furthermore, Roberts contends, the future success of white men is threatened by quota systems in education and employment that emphasize minority-group rights over individual merit.

As you read, consider the following questions:
1. According to Roberts, why are white males denied "victim status"?
2. In Roberts's opinion, what historical facts reveal that white males have gotten "a bum rap"?

From Paul Craig Roberts, "Demonization of the White Male," *Washington Times*, January 5, 1996. Reprinted by permission of the *Washington Times*.

W hite males are now officially declasse. The proof is the appearance of a new lapel button that reads: "Some of my best friends are white males."

The delegitimization—even demonization—of the white male has reached extreme lengths. The rhetoric is comparable to Marxism's demonization of class enemies and the denunciation of Jewry by anti-Semites.

For example, Syracuse University Professor Laurence Thomas says that "white males have committed more evil cumulatively than any other class of people in the world," and University of Pennsylvania Professor Houston Baker declares "white males" to be history's greatest criminals for perpetrating "the most globally insidious and unmercifully bloody manifestations of colonialism, imperialism, and racism" ever known.

That such offensive characterizations of white males are commonplace testifies to their loss of civil rights. Any such negative stereotyping of any other group would result in civil rights lawsuits. White males, however, are no longer protected by civil rights law. It is permissible—indeed necessary—to discriminate against them in order to give preferences to "protected minorities."

THE VICTIMS OF DEMONIZATION

It doesn't seem to bother anyone that white males are now second class citizens under the law. Fordham University Professor Mark Naison recently dismissed white males' loss of their civil rights as a mere inconvenience. The Republican Congress regards Medicare and welfare reform as more important than equality before the law and has taken no steps to reverse the institutionalized reverse discrimination that is the backbone of U.S. civil rights policy.

Today white males are the victims of discriminatory practices, but their demonization denies them victim status. Many have been intimidated into silence, and others accept their second class status as punishment for past "hegemonic" behavior.

The American white male has gotten a bum rap. It was American white males who abolished slavery, who gave women the vote, who desegregated the schools, who passed the 1964 Civil Rights Act. And it was conservative white males in the Nixon administration who established racial quotas and spread them across the country like Johnny Appleseed.

This record is the antithesis of "racist and sexist hegemony," but facts play no role in demonizations.

White males might not be able to get their civil rights back. There is no sympathy with their plight, and they are a minority.

Moreover, the preferences that every other group has are valuable, and the "protected minorities" that have them—a majority of the population—will want to keep them.

REVERSE DISCRIMINATION IN LOS ANGELES

Because of their skin color, "white," 5,000 applicants were prohibited from taking the firefighter exam in Los Angeles in February 1994. This injustice resulted from a 1974 consent decree between the city of Los Angeles and the Justice Department. The decree's interim and long-range goals effectively required the fire department to hire 50% of its firefighters from among minority groups.

A member of the Los Angeles Fire Commission, Michelle Eun Joo Park-Steel, declares that "Discrimination is against the fundamental values of American culture. It was wrong in the Jim Crow era and it is wrong 100 years later. . . . The old policies of rigid goals are insensitive to current, legitimate needs of all citizens. Hostility toward any race is no longer acceptable. If Los Angeles is to become safer and more prosperous, it must establish a world-class attitude that gives everyone an equal opportunity to serve our city."

Allan C. Brownfeld, *Human Events*, July 1, 1994.

White males are also disadvantaged by a change in philosophy. Merit is out, and civil rights is interpreted to require proportionately equal outcomes by race and gender. Since white males achieved disproportionately more success under the old merit system, they are still disproportionately represented in the workforce, management ranks, and professions. This disproportional representation is taken as proof of their race and gender hegemony.

A BLEAK FUTURE

Because individual merit has given way to group entitlement, the outlook is dim for white males. Parents following the traditional emphasis on hard work, good grades and proper behavior are setting many sons up for disillusionment when they find that meritocratic criteria are routinely trumped by quotas.

Conservatives seem helpless to address the demise of equality before the law or its transformation into equal outcomes. For example, Clint Bolick, who served in the Reagan administration, calls affirmative action a fraud in a 1996 pamphlet from the Cato Institute.

However, Mr. Bolick finds quotas fraudulent because they don't do enough to help poor blacks, not because they compromise the constitutional rights of white males. The implication of Mr. Bolick's critique is that racial quotas would be fine if they succeeded in bringing poor blacks into the economic mainstream and in integrating society.

Mr. Bolick has the "white man's burden" view: It is the job of whites as a group to do something that makes blacks as a group successful. Until whites succeed in this task, they are deserving of disapprobation.

Meanwhile, at California's Chico State University a dean advertised for a "dynamic teacher" who would not put students to sleep. He was overruled by the school's affirmative action director, who found the adjective "dynamic" to be "restrictive," "Euro-centric" and "phallo-centric."

It would be no less restrictive to advertise for a capable teacher or a competent one. All qualifications are restrictive— which explains their de-emphasis and the plight of overrepresented white males in our brave new world of equal outcomes.

| "White men still control virtually
everything in America."

WHITE MEN DO NOT FACE REVERSE DISCRIMINATION

Malik Miah

In the following viewpoint, Malik Miah contends that the claim of widespread reverse discrimination against white males is not valid. According to Miah, white men make up less than half of the workforce, but they still hold most of the management and skilled labor positions. Although many white males who have trouble finding work blame affirmative action, a weakening economy is the real reason for job loss among white men, he concludes. Miah is the managing editor of *Independent Politics*, a bimonthly socialist news magazine.

As you read, consider the following questions:

1. What is the main criterion for jobs and promotions in corporate America, according to Miah?
2. In the author's opinion, how does capitalism hold on to the loyalty of white workers?

From Malik Miah, "Class, Race, Sex, and the Angry White Male," *Independent Politics*, May/June 1995. Courtesy of the author.

"A great national debate on affirmative action is about to tear our nation apart," writes self-proclaimed white liberal Arthur Hoppe in a March 6, 1995, *San Francisco Chronicle* column. "We will all be asked to have the courage to take a side. I'm against it.

"All my life I've marched, voted, argued and written for racial equality, but I find myself against affirmative action programs based on the color of one's skin.

"I say this after looking back on my own life. *As far as my career goes, I would have had an easier time of it in many respects had I been Black.*" [emphasis added]

"Surely," he continues, "it's unfair to give the son of a Black banker preference over the son of a white sharecropper."

Although the overwhelming majority of Blacks are low-wage workers, the often-repeated lie that the Black middle class is taking over is perceived as the truth. Hoppe ends his piece, "I can share the anger of my younger white friends. They're as bitter at being discriminated against today as my Black friends have been for the past 400 years."

Really? Thirty years of affirmative action has produced a bitterness equal to that produced by over 200 years of slavery, followed by 100 years of Jim Crow segregation? White skin must be pretty thin.

Is Hoppe a "born-again" racist? Not yet. But he is an angry white male who thinks his sons will suffer as much from affirmative action as Blacks have suffered from racist discrimination.

Hoppe is not unique. There are many white male workers who believe in their bones that Blacks are getting a better shake than whites. They all have at least one example of someone who's Black getting ahead over a more qualified white.

The "New" Racists

The conservative offensive against affirmative action also has an ideological component. Published in 1994, *The Bell Curve* by Charles Murray and Richard Herrnstein gives the intellectual rationalization for the "new" racists. They proclaim a simple "fact": the source of inferior test scores, higher unemployment and other inequalities among African Americans is genetic. In other words, white men run the corporations because of better genes.

While few capitalist politicians would publicly support this racist theory, many believe it.

A government study puts the lie to the theory of "reverse discrimination." Issued on March 15, 1995, the "Glass Ceiling Commission" report states that there is a glass ceiling in corporate America. It found that white men, while constituting about 43 percent of the workforce, hold about 95 of every 100 senior management positions, defined as vice president and above. White women hold close to 40 percent of middle management jobs, Black women about 5 percent, and Black men hold 4 percent. Not surprisingly, working women still earn only 70 percent of what white males earn.

THE DENIAL OF RACISM

The real criterion for hiring and promotions in corporate America is what it has always been: connections. Robert Scheer, writing in the *San Francisco Chronicle* (March 26, 1995), quotes one white manager who "told the truth: that, in hiring, 'What's important is comfort, chemistry, relationships and collaborations.' That's why Black, college-educated professional men earn only 71 percent of the earnings of their white counterparts on the bell curve: The comfort level is too low." When a white man is passed over for promotion, it's because his white male bosses have to give the job to an "unqualified" woman or non-white man.

The same preferences apply to blue collar jobs. Skilled jobs are generally the private domain of white men. For example, in the airlines, it took legal action initiated by African Americans in the 1970s to force open mechanic and pilot jobs for Blacks and women. Court action benefited not only Blacks and women, however. In the case of United Airlines, a court-ordered consent decree modified the seniority system, making it easier for all workers to upgrade their skills—an example of affirmative action helping white males.

White men still control virtually everything in America. According to the Urban Institute, 53 percent of Black men aged 25 to 34 are either unemployed or earn too little to lift a family of four from poverty.

Writing in the *Nation* (March 27, 1995), Roger Wilkins compares the "denial of racism" to "denials that accompany addictions to alcohol, drugs or gambling. It is probably not stretching the analogy too much to suggest that many racist whites are so addicted to their unwarranted privileges and so threatened by the prospect of losing them that all kinds of defenses become acceptable, including insistent distortions of reality in the form of hypocrisy, lying or the most outrageous political demagogy.". . .

RULING CLASS CONCERNS

The potential for race conflicts is one reason the editors of the *New York Times* are opposed to attempts to roll back the modest affirmative action programs in place. In a February 28, 1995, editorial entitled "The Nuclear Wedge Issue," the editors wrote: "Citizens should not be deceived about the real motivation behind the gathering crusade against affirmative action. The rhetoric about reverse discrimination is the '90s equivalent of blue smoke and mirrors. Everyone in American politics knows what is going on, and if three decades of racial progress are to be abandoned, let us at least be candid about it. Republican strategists and the party's Presidential candidates have spotted a nuclear-strength wedge issue for the 1996 election."

© Kirk Anderson. Reprinted with permission.

Then they point to the reason for a possible nuclear explosion in race relations if the bigots and hypocrites get their way: "A growing economy once cushioned the impact of such [job] competition. But as high-salaried industrial and government jobs disappear, a sinister national tendency toward scapegoating has resurfaced. . . .

"Critics of affirmative action," they continue, "would have a strong case if their handful of reverse-discrimination examples represented a vast national problem. But the reality is far different, and it is an apotheosis of illogic to have the United States junk 30 years of progress because a Colorado contractor lost a $300,000 guard-rail contract to a minority bidder.

"Among doctors, lawyers, scientists and university teachers, fewer than one in 20 are Black," they add. "The ratio is only slightly higher in the construction trade. The plain truth is that the number of Blacks at the professional or skilled labor levels is simply too slight to produce much competition, let alone discrimination against white men.". . . .

WHITE MALES ARE PAWNS

U.S. capitalism cannot offer white workers the same standard of living and security that most of their parents enjoyed. But capitalist politicians and the big-business press will not admit that corporate greed and the unending drive for higher profits are the forces squeezing white workers and their families. Scapegoating affirmative action programs is capitalism's ideological tool for holding onto the allegiance of white workers. . . .

Institutional racism and sexism, rooted in capitalism, are behind the polarization between races and the much deeper class divisions. White males are the pawns of the rich and powerful who reap super profits by fostering and reinforcing past and existing social conflicts. White men are told to circle the wagons around their ethnic group to protect "their" jobs and security against those perceived as inferior, as threatening their "rightful" privileges.

How to bust this insidious circle? It requires action—special forceful steps by the government and employers to level the playing field so objective criteria (related to real "merit") are used to determine who gets what job or promotion, and not "connections" alone.

| "Liberals so monopolize the market-
place of opinion because of their
domination of the media, the arts,
and the schools, . . . [that] they just
declare other viewpoints off limits."

POLITICAL CORRECTNESS FOSTERS
REVERSE DISCRIMINATION

Rush H. Limbaugh III

Liberal educational and social policies that advocate sensitivity
about race and gender issues are often described as "politically
correct." Many people believe that political correctness has become a nationwide movement that advocates censoring opinions and behaviors considered to be offensive to minorities,
women, homosexuals, and other groups. In the following viewpoint, Rush H. Limbaugh III asserts that political correctness
limits free speech and leads to the victimization of people
wrongly accused of racism and bigotry. Moreover, Limbaugh
contends, overt offenses against conservatives and white males
often go unpunished, allowing reverse discrimination to flourish. Limbaugh is the host of a nationally syndicated radio talk
show. The following viewpoint is excerpted from his book *See, I
Told You So*.

As you read, consider the following questions:

1. What comparison does Limbaugh make between political
   correctness and ethnic cleansing?
2. In Limbaugh's opinion, how do "hate crime" laws violate
   freedom of speech?
3. What examples does the author give to support his
   contention that political correctness has gone too far?

W hat have I been telling you people about "political correctness"? Have I not told you about the threat this poses to free expression and the constitutional limits on government? Well, my friends, things just got a little bit worse.

In fact, for all intents and purposes, "political correctness," in my opinion, is now an obsolete term. It is far too polite and genteel a label to describe the brand of political oppression being imposed on certain kinds of thought in this country. From now on, let's call it what it is: thought control and "political cleansing."

Why do I call it "political cleansing"? When the Serbs launched a genocidal scorched-Earth policy against the Muslim population in Bosnia, it was characterized as "ethnic cleansing." Liberals are up to the same thing—only instead of wiping out a people, they are targeting certain ideas and viewpoints. Liberals so monopolize the marketplace of opinion because of their domination of the media, the arts, and the schools, that some of them have come to believe that their pet theories and beloved philosophical constructs have no legitimate intellectual competition, so they just declare other viewpoints off limits. That's what I mean by "political cleansing."

The hypocrisy of it is palpable. The left-wing thought police are forever paying lip service to the ideals of free expression, but they are the first ones in line to place restrictions on it for those with whom they disagree.

"HATE CRIMES" REQUIRE THOUGHT POLICE

Take Texas governor Ann "Ma" Richards. . . . In 1993, she signed into law a bill that enhances penalties for "bias-motivated crimes." Here's how it works: If you killed someone in Texas for the sheer sport of it, or because you wanted to steal the person's money, or because you got up on the wrong side of the bed that morning, you would be punished less severely than a murderer who killed because he was a bigot. In Texas, for instance, murderers who are motivated by bigotry and prejudice cannot be paroled, as can your normal, run-of-the-mill killer.

But it won't be just Texans who are subject to this kind of double standard of justice. A few days before "Ma" Richards signed her legislation, the U.S. Supreme Court opened the door for laws like it throughout the United States by holding that they pass constitutional muster.

Let's analyze this. Do you know what constitutes a "hate crime"? Put your thinking caps on. What tools do we need to determine whether a crime was motivated by hate or prejudice?

Answer: We need thought police.

Through the power of a Supreme Court ruling, and the actions of "Ma" Richards and the Texas legislature, America has legitimized thought police. Our Anglo-American system of criminal law has always sanctioned the grading of offenses based on the actor's state of mind or criminal intent (referred to by the legal profession as *mens rea*). For example, negligent homicide constitutes involuntary manslaughter in most jurisdictions and is punishable far less severely than premeditated murder is. The criminal's state of mind, in terms of whether he intended to do it and planned it in advance, has always been deemed legally relevant in terms of grading the offense and the culpability of the criminal. But for the first time in our history of jurisprudence, with the full blessing of the Supreme Court, we are going to allow state legislatures to grade criminal offenses based on "why" a person committed the crime.

"But, Rush," some people will say, "it's wrong to be biased. It's bad to hate. It's not nice to be bigoted. Why not punish these people more?"

I agree that hating is wrong. Bigotry is bad. But until now, harboring these feelings has not been a crime. We've just made it a crime to express a bigoted thought. We've just made it a crime to hate. Quite literally, what we are doing is violating freedom of speech. The First Amendment of the Constitution of the United States has just been infringed.

THE PROBLEM WITH LIBERAL RHETORIC

Let's analyze this further. If burning a flag is protected speech, as opposed to conduct, then a bigoted state of mind accompanying a killing should be entitled to First Amendment protection as well (not the killing itself, but the inquiry into why).

Let's get to the real root of this. What we have at work here is vintage liberalism. Liberals refer to these crimes born of a bigoted mind-set as "hate crimes." The ostensible rationale for grading the offense more seriously is that a person is more culpable if he committed a crime out of hatred. But hold on. That's not it at all. Let's look beyond the impassioned liberal rhetoric for a moment. What about someone who, upon learning that his mother has been murdered, immediately kills her murderer? Is it not safe to assume that the murdering son's crime was motivated by hatred? Of course. But how does the law treat this man? How should it treat him? The answer is that if he committed the crime soon enough following the provocation, while still in the throes of passion and before having had time to cool off, his crime may be reduced from first- or second-degree murder to voluntary manslaughter and punished less severely. It is reduced because of his "adequate provocation."

How can a liberal explain the difference? Both the bigoted murder and the murder committed by the son are born of hatred, yet one may actually receive a *lesser* sentence. . . .

POLITICAL CORRECTNESS ON CAMPUS

There are at least five areas to which PC applies and where it succeeded in imposing a fair amount of conformity. They are: 1) race-minority relations; 2) sexual and gender relations; 3) homosexuality; 4) American society as a whole; 5) Western culture and values. In regard to each, PC prescribes publicly acceptable opinions and attitudes which are often conveyed on the campuses by required courses, freshman orientation, sensitivity training, memoranda by administrators, speech codes, harassment codes, official and student publications and other means.

Deviation from the norms of PC may result in public abuse, ostracism, formal or informal sanctions, administrative reproach, delayed promotion, difficulty of finding a job, being sentenced to sensitivity training, etc. Unlike in the 1960s, of late the pressure to conform to left-liberal beliefs (the essence of PC) arises from the administration and groups of faculty (usually of the '60s generation of former radicals, concentrated in the humanities and social sciences) rather than from student radicals.

Paul Hollander, *Washington Times*, December 28, 1993.

The plain and simple answer, folks, is that liberals couldn't care less whether a crime is committed with hatred—unless the hatred is of a politically incorrect variety. If a murderer commits a crime based on his hatred of African Americans, Native Americans, homosexuals, probably even pornographers, he is committing a hate crime that is deserving of more severe punishment than if he murders because he hates white males or right-wing evangelists, for example. . . .

THE TYRANNY OF LIBERAL VIEWS

If government can make it a crime to be a racist or a bigot, why not criminalize other viewpoints? Don't be fooled by the argument that this is not an infringement of free expression because the thought is coupled with a criminal act and it is the act that is being punished. Wrong. The thought itself that accompanies that act is what aggravates the penalty under these bizarre statutes. This is the insidious way the thought police can get their feet in the door to impose the tyranny of their views on the rest of society through the awesome enforcement authority of the criminal justice system. How long will it be before governments decide to make it illegal, let's say, to oppose abortion, or war, or homosexuality? These issues, just as with racism, prompt people to take political and moral positions. After all, what's unique about racist or bigoted viewpoints? Why should they be the only immoral positions to be criminalized? I fear the floodgates have been opened.

I have to disagree with Chief Justice William Rehnquist's opinion on this matter. He wrote that these laws are especially needed because bias crimes are "thought to inflict greater individual and societal harm. Its victims suffer distinct emotional harm more damaging than other victims." I beg to differ. Victims are victims. A murder victim is not less dead, nor more dead, because his killer murdered him in a state of bigoted passion. If I get mugged today by a guy who just wants my money, why should he get less of a sentence than a guy who mugged me because he doesn't like radio talk-show hosts? But that's the kind of thing that could happen with this new category of crime. . . .

Okay, maybe you're not worried about these laws because you're a law-abiding citizen and they're geared only toward punishing criminals. Fair enough. But these laws have implications for the way we all interact with one another. Hate-crime laws are merely the latest and most blatant manifestation of government creating a new category of thought crimes or infractions. But there are others that are victimizing perfectly innocent, law-abiding citizens.

Imagine, for instance, that you're a hard-working, mind-your-own-business, nose-to-the-grindstone student at the University of Pennsylvania. You have done nothing wrong, but you get a call to report to the judicial inquiry office. There you're told that the university wants to place in your permanent transcript a warning that you are a "racial harasser."

"There is no feeling worse than being completely, unjustly accused of racism," said Eden Jacobowitz, the victim of this witch-hunt. Believe me, Eden, I know.

WRONGLY ACCUSED OF HARASSMENT

This is a real-life story. This is not "theory." This is the way political cleansing and thought control affect innocent people in the real world. Listen to Jacobowitz's story. This is an excerpt from a letter he sent me after he was accused of racial harassment:

On Wednesday night, January 13, 1993, members of a sorority were outside my window stomping their feet, and making a "woo-woo" noise, and shouting and singing at an extremely loud and noisy level. It was almost midnight and I was trying to study. I went to the window and shouted, "Shut up, you water buffalo!" And since they were singing something about a party, I said, "If you're looking for a party, there's a zoo a mile from here."

Later, racial-harassment charges were brought against me because the sorority women were black. True, I knew the color of their skin, but it was a matter of absolute indifference to me. All I cared about was the fact that I was trying to study and my concentration was completely disrupted by extremely loud stomping and shouting.

The next thing I knew, police came by the dormitory asking questions. Knowing I didn't do anything that actually should concern the police, I volunteered my information to them. Other people were shouting curses and racial slurs out their windows the same time I was shouting the things I was shouting, but all I shouted was "water buffalo." I thought this would be the last I heard about this case, but I couldn't have been more wrong.

The police came by the next morning and I skipped class to talk to them. On that day I offered to speak to the women to explain my truly harmless intentions, but this was never granted to me, not by the police and not by the judicial inquiry office. The next day, January 15, I told President [Sheldon] Hackney about the entire incident, asking him to make sure that this case does not turn into one where the defendant is considered guilty from the second he's accused only because the case is under racial-harassment policy. . . .

I was notified by Robin Reed, an assistant judicial inquiry officer, that the case had been assigned to her, and she would conduct the investigation. . . . She decided that by my words I meant "big black animals that live in Africa." She decided that that's what water buffalo are—big black animals that live in Africa. Well, first of all, Mr. Limbaugh, water buffalo are indigenous to Asia. Second of all, that was the furthest meaning from my mind. "Water buffalo" described the noise they were making and is a direct English translation of the Hebrew word *behema*, which as slang simply means "fool." This word is used from Jew to Jew and has absolutely no racial connotations.

Of course, Sheldon Hackney, the man who presided over this fiasco of injustice, is not just the president of the University of Pennsylvania. He is also the husband of a friend of Hillary Clinton's and was, at the time, President Bill Clinton's nominee to head the National Endowment for the Humanities. That's why, I believe, confidentiality was critical to pushing the case against Jacobowitz. Perhaps the university tried to delay the student's hearing so as not to jeopardize Hackney's confirmation as head of the NEH. (He was confirmed in late July 1993.)

When that strategy failed, and syndicated columnists, the *Wall Street Journal* editorial page, and yours truly began crusading on behalf of Jacobowitz, the case was mysteriously dropped. The official story is that the "water buffalo" in question decided not to pursue the matter further. Why? Because, they said, the media attention would prevent them from having a fair hearing. Imagine that! I'm more than a bit skeptical. The only thing fair about this whole incident was the fact that the light of truth was able to shine on it. I can only speculate that perhaps Sheldon Hackney went to the "water buffalo" and said, "Listen, you can't win this thing. And I want that job at the National Endowment for the Humanities."

SOME HAVE FEWER RIGHTS THAN OTHERS

But look at all the media attention that was required before common sense prevailed at the university. And what would have happened had the president of the institution not been up for a high-profile government post? Eden Jacobowitz, a very decent young man, probably would have been shafted. And how many more Eden Jacobowitzes are there out there? And how many Sheldon Hackneys?

This was not Hackney's only contribution to the doctrine of political cleansing. While Eden Jacobowitz was being hung out to dry, 14,000 copies of the campus newspaper, the *Daily Pennsylvanian*, were taken and destroyed by a group of black students protesting what they saw as "blatant . . . perpetuation of institutional racism" by the paper and a conservative columnist.

What did Hackney do about it at the time? He issued a namby-pamby, feel-good statement that "two important university values, diversity and open expression, seem to be in conflict." I guess he thought "diversity" was being promoted by virtue of the "open expression" inherent in destroying 14,000 newspapers. And that was the end of it. Mind you, there was no talk about a hate crime. This works only in one direction. Because for the politically correct crowd, hatred of white males and/or conservatives cannot by definition be racist. It is a justifiable emotion based on centuries of discrimination and other evils perpetrated by white males. But, in the past, Hackney has adamantly defended free speech—or at least liberal free speech. When homosexual activists chalked sexually explicit and anti-religious graffiti on a campus sidewalk, Hackney ensured that maintenance workers were forbidden from washing it off in the interest of free expression. He stood up for a campus appearance by the racist Louis Farrakhan, minister, Nation of Islam. And he backed the National Endowment for the Arts in subsidizing sexually explicit and anti-religious artwork with federal taxpayer dollars. This is not a man trying to avoid controversy. This is a man with an ideological axe to grind. According to the Sheldon Hackneys of the world, we all have a right to open expression, but some have less rights than others.

> "The conservatives aren't really victims. They are still the same privileged people they have always been."

POLITICAL CORRECTNESS IS A CONSERVATIVE MYTH

John K. Wilson

Calls to limit behavior or speech considered to be offensive to minorities have become controversial on college campuses because many people believe such efforts have grown into a movement—"political correctness"—that suppresses free thought and open dialogue. In the following viewpoint, John K. Wilson asserts that this political correctness movement is merely a myth promoted by conservatives to discredit liberal ideals. In an attempt to silence concerns about racial injustice, he contends, conservatives have exaggerated the effects of political correctness and have claimed that politically correct policies unfairly oppress conservative white males. Wilson is the author of *The Myth of Political Correctness: The Conservative Attack on Higher Education*, from which the following viewpoint is excerpted.

As you read, consider the following questions:
1. What is the origin of the phrase "political correctness," according to Wilson?
2. In what ways has political correctness been blamed for media censorship, in Wilson's opinion?
3. According to the author, in what ways have conservatives declared themselves to be victims of political correctness?

In 1991, a new phrase began to be heard across America. *Political correctness*, PC for short, quickly became one of the hottest terms in the country, spawning a flood of books, magazine articles, and editorials describing a reign of terror at American universities, led by radical students and faculty and supported by acquiescent administrators. Within the span of a few months, the media produced a barrage of articles, each a variation on a single theme: that leftist totalitarians had taken control of universities and were intimidating professors, censoring conservatives, politicizing curricula, and imposing a new "McCarthyism of the Left" on higher education.

"Political correctness" became the rallying cry of the conservative critics of academia, the phrase behind which all of their enemies—multiculturalism, affirmative action, speech codes, feminism, and tenured radicals—could be united into a single conspiracy. The mythology of political correctness declares that conservatives are the victims of a prevailing leftist ideology in American universities, oppressed by radical students and faculty determined to brainwash them. But the conservative attacks on these politically correct "thought police" have distorted the truth about what goes on in colleges and universities. Instead of condemning the excesses of a few extremists and abuses of due process by administrators, critics have declared that the mere presence of radical ideas has corrupted the entire system of higher education. Instead of telling the truth, the forces against political correctness have used exaggeration and distortion to create the mythology of PC, a myth that bears little resemblance to what is really happening on college campuses.

A CONSPIRACY OF LEFTISTS?

Conservatives manufactured the political correctness crisis and skillfully pushed it into the national spotlight. This does not mean that all examples of political correctness are pure invention; leftists do sometimes show intolerance toward those who fail to toe the party line. But leftist intimidation in universities has always paled in comparison with the far more common repression by the conservative forces who control the budgets and run colleges and universities.

My claim is not that American universities are perfect defenders of free expression, or that political correctness is pure invention with no basis in reality. When I describe political correctness as a myth, I do not mean that everything about it is false or every anecdote is fraudulent. Walter Lippmann once noted that "the distinguishing mark of a myth is that truth and error, fact and fable, report and fantasy, are all on the same plane of credibility." Without doubt many students and faculty have been wrongly punished for their views. And there are some leftists who would not hesitate, if given the power, to oppress conservatives. But generally they do not have the power, and few have the inclination to create their own ideological monarchies. The greater power is held by the status quo, which often enforces conservative doctrines without ever gaining the publicity devoted to leftist PC.

UNIVERSITIES ARE CONVENTIONAL

For some time now, we have been asked to believe that higher education is being devalued by the "politically correct" tyrannies of feminists, African-American nationalists, gays, lesbians, and Marxists. The truth is something else. In fact, most college professors and students are drearily conventional in their ideological proclivities. And the system of rule within the average university or college, be it private or public, owes more to Sparta than to Athens. The university is a chartered corporation ruled, like any other corporation, by a self-appointed, self-perpetuating board of trustees, composed overwhelmingly of affluent and conservative businesspeople.

Michael Parenti, Humanist, September/October 1995.

The myth of political correctness has created the illusion of a conspiracy of leftists who have taken over higher education and twisted it to serve their political purposes. Attacks on political correctness have misled the public and unfairly maligned a large number of faculty and students. Worse yet, the crusade against PC has silenced the deeper questions about quality and equality that our colleges and universities must face, and a greatly needed debate has been shut down by the false reports and misleading attacks on higher education. The myth of political correctness has made every radical idea, no matter how trivial or harmless, seem like the coming of an apocalypse for higher education, complete with four new horsepeople—Speech Codes, Multiculturalism, Sexual Correctness, and Affirmative Action.

The conservative backlash against universities has been funded by right-wing foundations and supported by liberals and journalists who dislike the academic Left. Using a long list of inaccurate anecdotes, endlessly recycled in conservative and mainstream publications, the right-wingers have distorted and manipulated the debates about higher education. Presenting conservative white males as the true victims of oppression on campus, they have convinced the public that radicals are now the ones who threaten civil liberties. This is the myth of political correctness that conservatives have created and successfully marketed to the media and the general public. . . .

The myth of political correctness has become accepted as gospel when describing the state of American universities. But the myth did not appear out of nowhere. It is the product of a conservative movement that undermined higher education throughout the Reagan-Bush years, honing its skills and funding the attacks that led to the PC bashing. The story of how "political correctness" began, and how conservatives used the myth of political correctness to appeal to liberals and journalists, reveals how little of the truth has really been told.

THE ORIGINS OF POLITICAL CORRECTNESS

In only a few years, the term *political correctness* has grown from obscurity to national prominence. The words first appeared two centuries ago in the 1793 Supreme Court case *Chisholm v. Georgia*, which upheld the right of a citizen to sue another state. Justice James Wilson wrote an opinion in which he objected to the wording of a common toast: "'The United States' instead of the 'People of the United States' is the toast given. This is not politically correct." Wilson's use of the term was quite literal. He felt that the people, not the states, held the true authority of the United States, and therefore a toast to the states violated the "correct" political theory. Supporters of states' rights did not concur, and the Eleventh Amendment was passed to overturn the *Chisholm* decision. And the phrase *politically correct* quickly faded from memory.

Although no one is sure when or where *politically correct* was revived, nearly everyone agrees that it was used sarcastically among leftists to criticize themselves for taking radical doctrines to absurd extremes. Roger Geiger notes that political correctness was "a sarcastic reference to adherence to the party line by American communists in the 1930s." Herbert Kohl "first heard the phrase 'politically correct' in the late 1940s in reference to political debates between socialists and members of the United States Communist Party," where "politically correct" was "being used disparagingly to refer to someone whose loyalty to the CP line overrode compassion and led to bad politics." Ruth Perry traces PC to the late 1960s and the Black Power movement, perhaps inspired by Mao Tse-tung's frequent reference to "correct" ideas. "Politically correct" was used not by extremists on the left to describe their enemies but by more moderate liberals who objected to the intolerance of some leftists. Perry says that "the phrase politically correct has always been double-edged" and "has long been our own term of self-criticism."

During the 1980s, conservatives began to take over this leftist phrase and exploit it for political gain, expanding its meaning to include anyone who expressed radical sentiments. Conservative writer Robert Kelner first heard of "political correctness" in the fall of 1985 as "a bit of college slang bandied about by young conservatives." And the conservatives not only appropriated *politically correct* for their own attacks on the radical Left, they also transformed it into a new phrase—*political correctness*. . . .

THE MAKING OF THE MYTH

In the 1990s, "political correctness" permeates our culture like no other soundbite of recent times. Although the debate in the universities has subsided somewhat, the phrase *politically correct* regularly appears on T-shirts and in newspaper headlines, TV shows, comic strips, and everyday conversations. The fear of being PC often reaches ridiculous proportions. In 1994, the Wilmette, Illinois, village board decided not to put a drawing of four children of different races on its village vehicle sticker because "it would take 'political correctness' too far" and would be "forcing people to promote diversity" in that nearly all-white suburb of Chicago.

"Political correctness" is a label slapped on an enormous range of liberal views—from environmentalism to multiculturalism to abortion rights. According to one writer, "It is P.C. to be in favor of affirmative action" and to "profess a belief in environmentalism, Palestinian self-determination, third world revolutionaries, and legalized abortion." By this definition, 90 percent of America is politically correct, which makes one wonder who's listening to Rush Limbaugh. Speaking of Rush, you can't read his books without being inundated with the phrase—he calls political correctness "the greatest threat to the First Amendment in our history," transcending wartime censorship and McCarthyism. Altogether, Rush invokes PC at least twenty-five times in his book *See, I Told You So*, including in two chapter titles. In "Political Correctness and the Coming of the Thought Police," Rush calls PC "political cleansing" akin to Serbia's "genocidal scorched-Earth policy against the Muslim population in Bosnia."

Political correctness even gets blamed for the censorship committed by its worst enemy, the religious Right. *Time* warns us that "under the watchful eye of the p.c. police, mainstream culture has become cautious, sanitized, scared of its own shadow. Network TV, targeted by antiviolence crusaders and nervous about offending advertisers, has purged itself of what little edge and controversy it once had." But virtually the only ones to protest TV shows and organize advertiser boycotts are right-wing groups who object to the depiction of homosexuality and other such "antifamily" material. The religious Right—not the PC Left—has been at the forefront of efforts to purge offensive elements from movies, music, and television, ranging from The Last Temptation of Christ to 2 Live Crew to NYPD Blue.

It isn't hard to learn that one can escape responsibility by yelling "PC" as loud as possible. James "Pate" Philip, the Republican president of the Illinois Senate, said to a newspaper editorial board about black social workers, "Some of them do not have the work ethics that we have . . . they don't tend to turn on or squeal on their fellow minorities." Philip—who easily won reelection in his district and was reelected by the Senate GOP caucus as their leader—justified his remarks by proudly declaring, "I'm not politically correct, I don't try to be." William Cash, who wrote a 1994 article about Hollywood's "Jewish cabal" in the British magazine Spectator, claimed it was "politically correct" to ignore this "Jewish influence." The Spectator's editor defended his decision to run the anti-Semitic essay by observing that "American papers have a code of political correctness.". . .

THE MYTH OF THE CONSERVATIVE VICTIM

The conservatives gained a major strategic victory in the culture wars when they declared themselves to be the oppressed rather than the oppressors. Instead of attacking Marxist professors and urging students to become spies as [the conservative watchdog group] Accuracy in Academia did [in the 1980s], conservatives in the 1990s present themselves as the victims of false charges of racism and sexism, victims of the repressive thought police, and victims of reverse discrimination. The critics of political correctness invert reality by declaring themselves oppressed by feminists and minorities. While sarcastically attacking "the victim's revolution" of minorities on campus, Dinesh D'Souza and other critics have created their own victim's revolution with a new victim: the oppressed conservative white male. D'Souza's book Illiberal Education tells the stories of various conservatives victimized by tenured radicals and student activists, including the ultimate victims of PC: the Dead White European Males of Western Civilization.

The conservatives' self-declared "victimization" is displayed by Robert Weissberg, a political scientist at the University of Illinois. Weissberg, writing to his fellow conservatives, declares: "We are the queers of the 1990s." Continuing his analogy, Weissberg says conservatives try to "pass" and fear a "public outing" of their views, since being called a conservative is "not all that different than, say, 'Richard Speck, Mass Murderer.'"

Even the rhetoric of the Left is being taken over by these "victimized" conservatives. "Young white men feel oppressed," the editor of *Reason* magazine says. "They have spent their entire lives officially marked 'undesirable.'" A conservative newspaper announced an "Oppressed Faculty Contest" sponsored by the Young America's Foundation, to award the $10,000 Engalitcheff Prize to a "college faculty member who swims against the prevailing stream of political correctness and intolerance." *American Spectator* founded a public service group, Amnesty in Academia, to defend the rights of faculty and students. It established a toll-free hotline to "report human rights violations on your campus" such as "the brutal interrogation of a student caught whistling the National Anthem on campus." Russell Jacoby, who examined the "human rights violations" Amnesty in Academia protested, concluded that they were merely "fictitious tales of fired university professors."

"Since our newfound sensitivity decrees that only the victim shall be the hero," Robert Hughes notes in *Time*, "the white American male starts bawling for victim status, too." Hughes would have us give up the idea of victims altogether and ignore the women who face sexism, the minorities subjected to racism, and the gays and lesbians vilified and attacked. Removing victims erases both American history and current realities, replacing them with a myth of justice and equality, in which bland declarations of our ideals conceal the fact that the noble aim of equal opportunity has never been achieved. The difference between the old victims and the new conservative white male victims is that the conservatives aren't really victims. They are still the same privileged people they have always been.

PERIODICAL BIBLIOGRAPHY

The following articles have been selected to supplement the diverse views presented in this chapter. Addresses are provided for periodicals not indexed in the *Readers' Guide to Periodical Literature*, the *Alternative Press Index*, the *Social Sciences Index*, or the *Index to Legal Periodicals and Books*.

Theodore William Allen	"Be Fair: Reverse Discrimination," *Z Magazine*, June 1995.
Michael M. Bowden	"Political Correctness and the First Amendment: The False Threat," *ABA Journal*, September 1993.
Economist	"AA: But Some Are More Equal than Others," April 15, 1995.
David Gates	"White Male Paranoia," *Newsweek*, March 29, 1993.
June Jordan	"Justice at Risk," *Progressive*, April 1996.
Michael S. Kimmel	"Invisible Masculinity," *Society*, September/October 1993.
Gerald F. Kreyche	"Time to Cry 'Auntie!'" *USA Today*, March 1993.
Michael J. Laird	"The Constitutionality of Political Correctness," *Communications and the Law*, September 1994.
John Leo	"The Demonizing of White Men," *U.S. News & World Report*, April 26, 1993.
Mari J. Matsuda and Charles R. Lawrence	"Myths About Minorities," *New York Times*, April 2, 1996.
Carl Mollins	"A White Male Backlash," *Maclean's*, March 20, 1995.
New York Times	"The Next-to-Last Word on Political Correctness," December 11, 1993.
Michael Parenti	"The Myth of the Liberal Campus," *Humanist*, September 1995.
Adolph Reed Jr.	"Assault on Affirmative Action," *Progressive*, June 1995.
Paul Craig Roberts and Lawrence M. Stratton	"Proliferation of Privilege," *National Review*, November 6, 1995.

CHAPTER 4

How Can Society Put an End to Discrimination?

CHAPTER PREFACE

In December 1992, the president of Santa Cruz Operation Incorporated (SCO), a California software company, was sued for sexual harassment by four secretaries. According to journalist Joan Walsh, SCO's board of directors responded by initiating a companywide diversity-training program as an "answer to the public-relations and employee-morale crises that ensued."

Diversity-training programs became popular after a 1987 Labor Department report projected that after the year 2000, 85 percent of new employees in the United States would be women or minorities. The goal of such programs is to deter workplace racism and sexism by developing workers' appreciation of gender, ethnic, and racial differences. Diversity trainers use a number of tools—including discussions, films, games, and role-playing—to enhance workers' understanding of the problems faced by women and people of color. About two-thirds of major U.S. companies now run programs designed to stop sexual harassment, alleviate racial tensions, and reveal discriminatory practices.

Supporters of diversity programs argue that the training provides a necessary eye-opener. Tim, a white manager at SCO, maintains that diversity training "taught me that you can't assume a commonality of perception. Women and people of color have had very different experiences, and they may see things differently from me. Today, when I'm with a woman or a black person, I know they may feel things I'm not aware of."

Critics of diversity training, however, argue that such programs are often so emotionally charged that they actually increase gender- and race-related tensions in the workplace. Some workers complain, for example, that trainers spend too much time attacking white males, leaving these men feeling unfairly blamed and accused. Others contend that diversity training has had little or no effect on workplace discrimination. Training manager Gail Garrow quit her job at SCO because, she claims, the company continued to ignore pay and promotion inequities between male and female employees. According to Garrow, "Sex discrimination is a systemic problem at SCO, and it hasn't gotten better since the [diversity-training] initiative [began]."

The authors in the following chapter offer differing opinions on diversity training as well as other approaches to eliminating workplace, campus, and societal discrimination.

| "The challenge is to end the corrosive system of racial preferences that has evolved in our nation."

ENDING AFFIRMATIVE ACTION WOULD PROMOTE EQUAL OPPORTUNITY

Ward Connerly

In the following viewpoint, Ward Connerly argues that affirmative action, originally intended to provide equal opportunity for people of color and women, instead led to quotas and preferential treatment. He asserts that affirmative action is an outdated policy that does not allow individuals to advance by merit regardless of their race or gender and that has in some cases increased racial tensions. In Connerly's opinion, eliminating affirmative action is the best way to promote equal opportunity for all members of society. Connerly, a University of California regent, was the chairman of the campaign for the California Civil Rights Initiative, a successful 1996 ballot measure designed to end state-sanctioned affirmative action.

As you read, consider the following questions:

1. In Connerly's opinion, what were some of the positive aspects of affirmative action?
2. What changes in America's racial makeup have made affirmative action obsolete, in the author's opinion?
3. What problems do racial and gender preferences create for students applying to state universities, according to Connerly?

From Ward Connerly, "With Liberty and Justice for All," Heritage Lecture Series, no. 560, March 8, 1996. Reprinted by permission of The Heritage Foundation.

When we become citizens of this nation, at birth or otherwise, we get a warranty. That warranty is supposed to be honored by every government franchise in every village and hamlet of this nation. It is not transferable, and it is good for the life of the vehicle.

We are guaranteed the right to vote; the right to due process; the right to be free, not to be enslaved, as long as we conduct ourselves in accordance with the laws of our nation; and the right to equal treatment under the law, regardless of our race, color, sex, religion, or national origin. These are rights which attach to us as individuals, not as members of a group.

This warranty has not always been honored for some of us. Because of the color of our skin or the place whence we came, some of us were denied the right to vote; we were enslaved; we were denied due process; and the equal treatment granted to others was not ours to enjoy.

In my lifetime, I can give testimony to America's meaner instincts and their consequences upon my life. To reflect upon this nation's past, with my racial background, it is tempting . . . to devalue the warranty and to be embittered by those who would urge me to forget the past.

One need only invoke a few memories to become enraged and to feel entitled to all of the preferences that can be presented:
- Rosa Parks relegated to the back of the bus,
- Drinking fountains for "whites only,"
- Restrooms for "men," "women," and "colored,"
- George Wallace standing in the schoolhouse door saying "segregation now, segregation forever,"
- Images of black people being hosed in the streets simply because they demanded that the warranty be honored,
- And my thirty-year-old uncle being called "boy" by a ten-year-old white kid.

Because we were treated like animals, there are some who say "America owes us." But the past is a ghost that can destroy our future. It is dangerous to dwell upon it. To focus on America's mistakes is to disregard its virtues.

A Passion for Fairness

This nation has a passion for fairness. That passion is evidenced in our Constitution, in the Bill of Rights, in executive orders, in court decisions. But most of all, it courses through the arteries of our culture. Do unto others as you would have them do unto you" is the centerpiece of virtually all of our religious faiths. . . .

Our passion for fairness seeps out of every pore of our existence. Great leaders understand that passion. In his early days, when members of his own church were urging him to "cool it," Dr. Martin Luther King Jr. appealed to America's sense of fairness and morality. It was Dr. King's appeal to fairness that resonated throughout the land and inspired Americans of all races and colors to travel to the deep South and to put their lives on the line in defense of what they considered the right thing, the fair thing to do.

Affirmative action has its roots in that passion for fairness. When President Lyndon Johnson explained affirmative action to the nation [in 1966], it is significant that he said, "You can't bring a man to the starting line who has been hobbled by chains and expect him to run the race competitively." Fairness dictated that the nation pursue affirmative action to compensate black Americans for the wrong that had been done. Affirmative action was a technique for jump-starting the process of integrating black Americans into the fabric of American society, for changing the culture of America from an exclusive society into an inclusive one.

I believe affirmative action was meant to be temporary. It was meant to be a stronger dose of equal opportunity for individuals, and the prescription was intended to expire when the body politic had developed sufficient immunity to the virus of prejudice and discrimination. It was not meant to be a system of preferences that would harm innocent people. The rationale for affirmative action thirty years ago was a moral one.

Three decades later, affirmative action is permanent and firmly entrenched as a matter of public policy. It has its own constituency that is prepared to defend its continuation at any cost, not because of any moral imperative, but because it has become the battleground for a political and economic war that has racial self-interest as its centerpiece.

GROUP PREFERENCES ARE WRONG

Affirmative action, as most of us originally understood the term, enjoyed the support of a majority of Americans. Many Americans still support this concept as long as it does not involve preferences. Preferences, on the other hand, were wrong at the outset and are wrong today.

Affirmative action has become a system of racial preferences in my state. Jobs are solicited with explicit acknowledgment that we want a woman or an African-American or a Hispanic for this position. Contracts are set aside for certain groups, with the taxpayers paying what amounts to an affirmative action tax. This is the result of contractors who set up shell minority and women-owned businesses to front for white-owned businesses in order to benefit from the minority set-asides.

Wealthy sons and daughters of underrepresented minorities receive extra points on their admissions applications to the university, based solely on their race, while higher-achieving Asians and whites from lower-income families are turned away from the university. Families are forced to mortgage their homes to send their children out of state to an institution comparable to [the University of California at] Berkeley and UCLA. A racial matrix is used at most of our campuses which establishes a racial pecking order that distributes extra points on the basis of one's racial background.

When this nation began its use of affirmative action decades ago, America's racial landscape was rather clear. There was the dominant white majority and the oppressed black minority. Today, we have several dozen racial and ethnic categories in California. There is no dominant majority and there is no oppressed minority. Within a few years, the group which will numerically be the largest is Hispanic. Our racial tensions are no longer just black and white. They are black and Korean, black and Hispanic, white and Hispanic, Russian and Hispanic. Every conceivable racial conflict is present and lurking somewhere beneath the surface in California. How, then, do we decide who among us should receive a preference?

A direct product of our diversity is the emergence of a whole new set of racial configurations and problems which defy the old racial order. Yet affirmative action operates as if the old order was still in place, as if our racial dilemma was still black against white. . . .

EQUAL OPPORTUNITY EXISTS

California is as close as any society on the face of the Earth to being that promised land where racism is considered repulsive and has no place. But this promised land can become a battle zone if we allow the continued tribalization of California.

We can point with pride to the fact that [in 1996] the mayor of one of America's favorite cities, San Francisco, is a black man: Willie Brown. The mayor of one of the largest cities in the nation, Los Angeles, for years was a black man: Tom Bradley. Our two United States Senators are women. The mayor of our state capital is Hispanic: Joe Serna. Although I as a Republican don't always agree with the political judgment of my fellow Californians, I believe no one can dispute their egalitarian impulses. As one looks at California state government, for example, the conclusion is inescapable: Equal opportunity is now inbred. The cabinet of Governor Pete Wilson is nearly equally divided among men and women, and it only takes a casual meeting with any of them to confirm that raw talent, and not affirmative action, is the basis of that fact.

I am terrified at the prospect of what can become of us if we maintain our existing preference policies. In police departments, in fire departments, in middle-class homes throughout California, there is a growing perception that if I am white, I and my kids will not have an equal opportunity to succeed. No matter where it comes from, if anyone among us believes the warranty is not being honored, we have a duty to investigate the legitimacy of their complaint and to make it right if their complaint is proven to be valid.

Reprinted by permission of Chuck Asay and Creators Syndicate.

Throughout this debate, you will hear about blacks being stopped in white neighborhoods, about white women clutching their purses as black men approach, about the difficulty of black men getting a taxi in urban centers late at night, about the glass ceiling, about the lack of role models, about the percentage of black males in prison, and about the shortage of women in the Congress. All of these complaints warrant our attention, but none of them, no matter how true, justifies a suspension of that warranty that I talked about.

There are those who say that racism and sexism are not dead in America, and they are correct. But racism and sexism in our society do not justify our government giving a preference to Jose over Chang because Susan's father discriminated against Willie's father fifty years ago. Not in America.

If you are a student of history, you know that every now and then, the opportunity to alter the course of human events presents itself. Such is now the occasion for the people of this nation.

Every now and then, the challenge confronts us to step out from among the crowd to perform extraordinary acts. Such is the moment for the Republican Party.

THE NEED FOR A CIVIL RIGHTS INITIATIVE

The challenge is to end the corrosive system of racial preferences that has evolved in our nation, a system that has the potential to fatally damage the most fundamental values of our democracy, and to do so in a way that does not unleash the meaner instincts of some and the fears of others. The opportunity is to resume that noble journey of building an inclusive family of Americans in which men and women of all races and colors can work and play in harmony, with mutual respect and expecting nothing more than an equal opportunity to compete, and from that competition to build that more perfect union of which our forefathers dreamed.

The vehicle for this journey is the California Civil Rights Initiative. This initiative is simple and direct: No government agency shall discriminate against anyone on the basis of race, sex, or national origin, and no government agency shall give anyone preferential treatment for any of those reasons.

Two days ago [March 6, 1996], I appeared on a talk show with Congresswoman Maxine Waters. She argued that the California Civil Rights Initiative will create divisiveness. That may be true, but we are not the ones creating the divisiveness. Those who cling to the notion that preferences must continue are the ones responsible for dividing our society.

- Ask the student who works hard for four years to earn a 4.0 grade point average only to be denied admission to Berkeley or UCLA in favor of someone with a 3.0, merely because UC wants racial diversity, whether she thinks we are being divisive.
- Ask the poor Vietnamese student who is turned away from Berkeley or UC, Irvine, despite his high grades, in favor of a wealthy underrepresented minority whether he thinks we

are being divisive. Ask him whether he is satisfied with the explanation that we are getting too many Asians at those campuses.

- Ask the daughter of a third-generation Chinese-American family whether she thinks we are being divisive when we say that it is unfair for applicants who are in this country illegally to get a preference over her.
- Ask the parents of James Cook, one of only two California students admitted to Johns Hopkins University in 1994 only to be denied admission to UC San Diego medical school because he is white, whether they think we are being divisive. Ask them and thousands of other middle-class families, who are forced to take out $80,000 to $100,000 second mortgages on their homes to send their kids out of state to college because racial preferences prevent them from being able to attend UC, whether they think we are being divisive.
- Ask the high-achieving black or Chicano student who works hard and gains entry to college solely on the basis of his merit, but who then must endure the nagging question of whether he was admitted because of affirmative action, whether he thinks we are being divisive. Ask him whether he thinks it's fair that his accomplishments are devalued.

DIVISIVENESS THREATENS DEMOCRACY

Do we not believe it was divisive when those from an earlier period said that slavery is immoral and should be ended? Was it not divisive when our nation's people fought among themselves over this very issue? Was it not divisive when we sent troops into Montgomery and Selma, Alabama, to protect the rights of people like Rosa Parks and James Meredith to ensure their right to sit wherever they wanted on the bus and to attend a college that wasn't segregated?

Yes, those were divisive times. But the seeds of division are planted not by those of us who seek to eliminate racial and ethnic preferences; they are planted by those who believe that our skin color and gender and how we spell our last name should entitle us to the harvest of diversity—college admission, government employment, and contracts. . . .

I find it interesting that a nation which claims to have the heart to solve an ethnic war in Bosnia shouldn't have the stomach to prevent one here at home. If there is any lesson that we can learn from the rest of the world, it is that America's experiment with democracy will fail if we divide our people into racial enclaves and allocate jobs, contracts, and college educations on the basis of group identity. . . .

A SENSE OF FAIR PLAY

And so, my friends, we find ourselves poised at this moment in the life of a great people, trying to define the character of our nation. Throughout America, we are restructuring our institutions. Our nation is desperately trying to embrace policies which place greater reliance on the rights and responsibilities of individuals. The debate about affirmative action must be seen in that context.

This issue will define the political parties in our nation for generations to come. The challenge for Republicans will be to convince all Americans that preferences are not in the national best interest, that a preference for some means a loss of liberty and the pursuit of happiness for others. We have to convince black Americans, a group which has become addicted to the drug of a powerful central government, that their rights can be no more secure than anyone else's when we empower government to make decisions about people's lives on the basis of a government melanometer which measures melanin levels. None of our rights are secure in a game of racial self-interest.

I will never abandon my faith that America can become Ronald Reagan's "shining city on the hill," a society in which a person's gender or race or ethnic background are irrelevant in the transactions of their government. Let us not mourn the death of affirmative action. Instead, let us proclaim our belief that the spirit of equal opportunity, which affirmative action engendered, has become a permanent feature of America's social, economic, and political landscape. Let us have faith in our own sense of fair play.

"*Affirmative action by all of our principal institutions must be taken in order to integrate and liberate American society.*"

RETAINING AFFIRMATIVE ACTION WOULD PROMOTE EQUAL OPPORTUNITY

Jamin B. Raskin

Many critics of affirmative action oppose it as a system that establishes quotas and preferential treatment for minority groups while ignoring individual merit. In the following viewpoint, Jamin B. Raskin takes issue with this opinion, asserting that affirmative action is a small but necessary step toward eliminating discrimination against and recognizing the merit of minorities and women. Since "merit" reflects the values of those who define it, and since access to educational institutions and employment is largely controlled by white males, Raskin maintains, affirmative action is still necessary to ensure equal opportunity for minorities and women. Raskin, a professor of law and associate dean at American University's Washington College of Law, has written extensively on civil rights and racial issues.

As you read, consider the following questions:
1. According to Raskin, what were the findings of Elizabeth Dole's Glass Ceiling Commission?
2. In the author's opinion, what various kinds of "merit" might make a student qualified for law school?
3. Why is it impossible to make race, gender, and class consciousness irrelevant to the admissions process, in Raskin's opinion?

From Jamin B. Raskin, "Affirmative Action and Racial Reaction," Z *Magazine*, May 1995. Reprinted by permission of the author.

The assault on affirmative action is the logical culmination of the popular campaign against "political correctness," which began in the late 1980s. The enemies of the thing called "PC" have enjoyed kicking around multiculturalism and deconstruction the last several years, but the real political energy behind the anti-PC campaign has always come from boiling white resentment over affirmative action. Now it is likely that the days are numbered for this exceedingly modest program to desegregate American life. . . .

The hysteria over affirmative action proceeds in the face of massive evidence of continuing white male dominance in society. The Glass Ceiling Commission, created by Elizabeth Dole when she was Secretary of Labor in the Bush administration, recently found that white men occupy 97 percent of senior management positions in Fortune 1000 and Fortune 500 corporations. African-Americans are found in about one-half of one percent of these top jobs, and there are even fewer Hispanics and Asian-Americans. In the private sector generally, African-Americans have just 2.5 percent of executive positions and black men who have professional degrees still earn less than four-fifths of the salaries earned by their white equivalents. Black women, facing double bias, earn three-fifths the amount that white men earn. Of course, African-Americans and other minorities, as well as women generally, form a greater presence in the public sector (one reason the public sector is in danger), but the ranks of top leadership are still almost all-white. There are no African-American governors in the United States, and out of 100 U.S. Senators, Carol Mosely Braun of Illinois is the only African-American.

THE COMPLAINT AGAINST AFFIRMATIVE ACTION

The complaint against affirmative action today boils down to the idea that "statist" university and government bureaucrats are compromising "traditional" and "historic" notions of "objective merit," "color-blindness" and "neutrality" by showing "preferential treatment" toward "unqualified" racial minorities and women. This "reverse discrimination" causes "unfairness" to that most victimized social group, white men, and, perhaps worst of all, "stigmatizes" its intended beneficiaries—minorities themselves. . . .

The critics of affirmative action invite us to believe that we live in a color-blind society in which the last vestige of racial discrimination is affirmative action itself. This extraordinary vision of American society simply cannot be squared with the facts of how whites and racial minorities live, how much they earn and what kind of wealth and power they have. The grim statistics of disparity force us to choose between the hideous *Bell Curve* vision of various races having differing aptitudes [*The Bell Curve* is a 1994 book that argues that different races have different intellectual abilities] and the far more plausible conclusion that different ethnic and racial communities have equal potential to flourish but different levels of access to wealth, power and the good life. Surely as a society we should choose the second interpretation as a matter of both empirical belief and moral faith. If we believe in the equal potential of all human beings and we therefore cannot justify the dominance of the "white race" over all others "in prestige, in achievements, in education, in wealth, and in power," in the words of Supreme Court justice John Marshall Harlan, then stepped-up race-conscious affirmative action by all of our principal institutions must be taken in order to integrate and liberate American society.

MERIT IS NOT EASILY DEFINED

This assertion, however, leads us directly to the the conservatives' central argument: that affirmative action undermines the regime of merit, which requires neutral distribution of social rewards according to objective criteria. Even just restating the argument begins to erode confidence in it because it is so obvious that each of its key terms is wholly empty outside of the process of historical definition. Merit is neither self-defining nor self-revealing; it is an ever-changing concept that is historically, socially and institutionally contingent—and often contested. It is impossible to define merit without asking what kinds of institutions we want to have and for what purposes. As Stanley Fish writes, "merit is not an abstract, independent standard but one that follows from the traditions and practices of a community whose presuppositions are not at the moment the object of scrutiny or skepticism." Once a particular conception of "merit" is challenged, it may be revised and transformed until the new conception is itself overthrown and the process repeats itself. The words that inevitably follow in the rhetorical train of "merit," such as "neutral" and "objective," are either totally abstract and empty or, in the real world, transparently loaded down with the freight of particular historical, social, political and institutional meanings.

Consider the example of law schools. A century ago, they had, roughly speaking, all-white, all-male faculties and all-white, all-male student bodies. The criteria then used for admission—race, gender, college attended, grades, family and social connections—worked to reproduce an elite bar that served the legal needs of emerging large-scale corporate capitalism. That system was not really altered until the Law School Admissions Test (LSAT) was introduced a few decades ago and agitation for social change lowered barriers for women and minorities to enter. At each step, voices were heard to say that neutral definitions of "merit" were being diluted in favor of some diluting trend.

Reprinted by permission of Mike Luckovich and Creators Syndicate.

But what qualities now warrant admission to law school? One can think of dozens: the extent to which a person would make an excellent brief-writer; the extent to which a person would make an excellent oral advocate; the extent to which a person would make a great legal scholar or great legal teacher; how well a person has performed on standardized exams, including the LSAT; the extent to which a person would enrich discussion in class; the extent to which the person has overcome adversity and demonstrates determination to succeed; the extent to which the person has empathy and compassion for people in vulnerable positions; the extent to which the person is part of a community in which she could find clients; how much business background a person has; the extent to which a person volunteers and serves others; the extent to which the person received good grades in college in law-related subjects; the quality of the application essays; the extent to which the person received good grades in college generally or in high school or in elementary school; the extent to which the person has worked during school, or worked in a law-related capacity; the extent to which the person is likely to go to a large law firm and give the law school large contributions as an alumnus; the extent to which the person will work to serve the poor and disempowered and thus bring recognition and praise to the law school; the extent to which a person will uplift an historically oppressed community through creative legal tactics—or keep it down through the same; the extent to which the person will use law to promote or undermine environmental protection; the extent to which the person has had the benefit (or hindrance) of coming from a family of lawyers or being the first person in her family even to apply to law school; and so on *ad infinitum.*

INSTITUTIONAL VALUE JUDGMENTS

Each of these criteria presents itself as a perfectly plausible consideration for law school admission today. How to choose among them? Surely it comes down to the school's self-definition and conscious (or unconscious) institutional project. But it is unlikely that any law school actually narrows its criteria down to just a few of these to the exclusion of all others. Rather, my experience has been that members of admissions committees tend to proceed on a series of general assumptions and hunches that incorporate all of these considerations and respond more or less idiosyncratically to the rationales for admission presented by an applicant's paperwork. Of course, many law schools place heaviest emphasis on college grades and LSAT scores but these should not be controlling criteria since neither is perfectly predictive of "success" and both are flawed in important ways. Of the two, grades appear to have a better capacity to predict "performance" in law school, but then again law school performance itself is defined with respect to grades, and who is to say that law students with better grades end up making better lawyers?

LSAT scores may best reflect whether the student took an LSAT preparation course, which are guaranteed to raise your score by 10 or 12 points or you get your money back. Of course, not everyone has the money or the time to take such a course. There are also a host of questions about whether a high-pressure, carefully timed competitive multiple-choice examination is the best way to test someone's ability to make a good and productive lawyer. The skills that permit someone to excel on such a test may predict how well they do on the bar exam or even how they would be as an associate at a large corporate law firm. But how well does excellence at taking the LSAT predict whether the person will work for justice, serve her community, exercise wisdom or change our way of looking at important legal issues?

Speaking personally, I favor a progressive lessening of reliance on the LSAT and a loosening of compulsive and unreflective attitudes about grades. But even schools that place most emphasis on the LSAT and grades do not use them exclusively; even they include room for discretion and judgment by admissions committee members. Thus, as soon as we stray from the illusive clarity of numerical criteria, we are thrown into the realm of value judgments about what kinds of institutions we want to create and what kinds of purposes we want them to serve. Is there something illegitimate about recognizing race, gender, ethnicity and socioeconomic background in this process?

No Escape from Race-Consciousness

The first point to make is that it is almost impossible not to take these factors into account without closing your eyes. When a law school applicant puts down on her application that she has spent the last three years raising her children, or that he spent twenty hours a week working his way through college, or that her parents are immigrants from Thailand, or that English is his second language, or that she was college vice-president of the Hispanic Students Association, or that she plans to work as a civil rights lawyer because her brother was a victim of race discrimination, or that she lives on an Indian reservation and plans to return there, then the complicated social facts of race, gender, class and ethnicity—which are partially constitutive of all of us as individuals—leap off the page and make themselves part of the consciousness of the admissions decision.

These facts that are so wrapped up with our selves cannot be blinked away; they inform admissions deliberations at every turn. If a student is poor, does his hard work as a pizza delivery person count in his favor or does the related fact that he had no meaningful extracurricular activities outside of work count against him? How should his summer delivering pizza be measured against a wealthier student's summer working as a paralegal at a law firm or volunteering at a homeless shelter? Does an applicant's knowledge of English as a second language suggest that law school will be too difficult for her or that she will be able to serve a lawyer-poor language minority community? Should a family full of lawyers be used to indicate likely success in law school and in finding a job or should it be used to discount the significance of the applicant's superb essay dealing with constitutional law? It is absurd to think that race, gender, and class ever were—or ever could be—"irrelevant" to the admissions process, which is all about making value judgments and deeply political choices. . . .

A DESIRE FOR SOCIAL CHANGE

In defending affirmative action, it is necessary to go beyond the idea of sharing power and resources in a culturally plural society. It is essential to recall the political and spiritual project of the modern Civil Rights movement that made affirmative action both necessary and possible. The Civil Rights movement never had as its conscious political project the creation of "affirmative action" or "set-aside" programs in various white-controlled institutions like universities, corporations, and labor unions. Affirmative action, rather, came about as part of the dominant society's effort to respond to the movement's growing insistence on fundamental social change to end oppressive conditions pervasive in the African-American community. . . .

It is a measure of both the vanishing of a popular energized Civil Rights movement and the nation's economic retraction that this modest program, seen as so unassuming and unobjectionable at the beginning, is now reviled in many places, deeply controversial and profoundly vulnerable. Thus, progressives who ought to be promoting far more radical proposals to reduce class power and race inequality in America are left holding the bag for a program designed by the establishment to assimilate social changes in a safe way and at a cautious speed. . . .

REVIVING AFFIRMATIVE ACTION

We need a defense of affirmative action that links up with a thoroughgoing critique of American meritocracy and power relationships. We need to revive a progressive challenge to the background social assumptions about education and employment in America: that higher education is for the elite only and should not be free to the people; that privately created and administered standardized exams are the best way to ascertain merit and distribute students across various levels of colleges; that the best teachers should teach the best students; that no one has a right to a job or productive work; that extreme hierarchy and role-division is inherent in the workplace; that radical disparities between the wages of people who handle things and people who handle words are natural and necessary; that work commonly done by women is inherently less worthy than work commonly done by men; that unions are an albatross and must be as authoritarian as employers; and that the society must operate on the principle of constant and fierce individual competition or else face ineluctable economic decline.

In short, to transcend the destructive politics of division and derision surrounding affirmative action (if we still can), we need to reaffirm the equality of all peoples in a culturally pluralist society and to posit a universal politics of freedom and equality for the next century. But a vigorous defense of affirmative action right now is central to such a politics. For in a society where the lines of race and gender double as lines of class and power, even the idea of affirmative action for minorities and women is an affront to the structure of domination and inequality. Our job must be to make affirmative action the first line of defense in a politics which insists that all citizens have a right to equal participation in the fruits of our social life.

| "Community dialogue can be a way both to demonstrate and to strengthen our will to become active in the task of dismantling racism."

DIVERSITY-TRAINING PROGRAMS ARE PRODUCTIVE

Andrea Ayvazian and Beverly Daniel Tatum

As a biracial team, Andrea Ayvazian and Beverly Daniel Tatum lead public forums and seminars on racism for Communitas Incorporated, a nonprofit organization that provides community diversity training and consultation. In the following viewpoint, Ayvazian and Tatum assert that diversity-training programs that promote dialogue between whites and people of color are an effective way to confront racial discrimination on a community level. Well-organized forums led by skilled facilitators can, in the authors' opinion, encourage honest, revealing, and empathetic discussion. Such dialogue, the authors contend, battles discrimination by helping people of different races to more fully understand each other as individuals. Ayvazian is the director of Communitas Incorporated in Northampton, Massachusetts. Tatum is an associate professor of psychology and education at Mount Holyoke College in South Hadley, Massachusetts. She is also the author of *Assimilation Blues: Black Families in a White Community*.

As you read, consider the following questions:

1. In the authors' opinion, why do whites tend to be less aware of racial issues than people of color are?
2. According to the authors, why is it difficult for most white people to listen to and believe people of color?
3. In Ayvazian and Tatum's opinion, how do caucus groups assist the process of community dialogue?

From Andrea Ayvazian and Beverly Daniel Tatum, "Can We Talk?" *Sojourners*, January/February 1996. Reprinted by permission of *Sojourners*.

An African-American woman notices that as she enters a room full of friends and colleagues—all white—the conversation stops when she walks through the door. An African-American man is routinely followed by the local police as he drives through a suburban community on his way to work. When he tells his white colleagues at work, his story is met with disbelief.

These vignettes are representative of the many stories we have heard as a biracial team that has provided hundreds of anti-racism training seminars and consultations nationwide. We ask people—white and of color—to talk about a subject that folks are usually careful to avoid: race relations and racism in the United States today.

With the O.J. Simpson verdict and the Million Man March [a 1995 mass meeting of African-American men in Washington, D.C.] behind us, the desire to avoid potentially painful and diffi-cult discussions has become even more intense. At the same time, many people are confused about why there is still such a deep racial divide in this country.

Recently in our travels, we have noticed that while people are reticent to discuss issues of race and racism in public, they pull us aside and ask us in whispered tones what we really think, or they explain their own theories to us behind closed doors. Even in these guarded conversations, we have been struck by a dis-cernible change in tone. Suddenly, it seems, white people are seeing the racial divide as looming larger than before. Race, so often dismissed by white people as an insignificant factor in contemporary U.S. society, has acquired meaning—meaning that they were working hard to ignore. There seems to be a veiled sense of panic in their conversation.

RACIAL WOUNDS

Because issues of injustice are always clearer from below, people of color have recognized the reality of racism for a very long time. But white America has enjoyed the dual luxuries of igno-rance and denial. Many whites have claimed—with a misplaced sense of pride—that they did not see color in friends, students, neighbors, or colleagues. In order to avoid confronting the dis-ease of racism, whites have clung to the myth of colorblindness. However, recent events have forced many whites to acknowl-edge that racism is still imbedded in the fabric of our society.

The nation is raw and divided—the racial wound is more vis-ible than it has been at any time since the civil rights movement and the urban riots of the 1960s. Just as we are hearing expres-sions of a quiet panic coming from whites in this country, the people of color we talk to are angry, and very cynical about white America's commitment to effecting significant change.

And yet, even against this backdrop of fear, anger, and cynicism, we believe that as a nation we have entered a period when the possibility for real change on the issue of racism is presenting itself. We believe that, as a people, we are at an important historical moment. The fact that racism has now surfaced so visibly once again gives us the opportunity to confront it directly, and to move forward in new and constructive ways.

Are we on the verge of a second wave of the civil rights movement? Maybe. We are unsure. What we are sure about is that we are hearing a level of concern, agitation, empowerment, and fear—along with a desire for dialogue—surrounding the issue of racism that we have not heard in the last 20 years.

THE NEED FOR PUBLIC DIALOGUE

If we are indeed at one of those rare moments when there exists the possibility for a significant paradigm shift, what can we do to seize this moment and move toward race equity in this country?

We believe the greatest need exists on the community level: the need for deep, honest, and ongoing public dialogue on race and racism between white people and people of color conducted in safe settings and in a structured fashion. Due to the level of segregation in our society, most white adults only interact with people of color at their workplace (if at all); their neighborhoods, houses of worship, and social circles remain predominantly white.

When we say that we need public dialogue on the community level about issues of race, we do not mean social events that encourage friendly mixing and polite conversation (although those may be useful as well). The public gatherings we are referring to would be specifically for the purpose of discussing race and racism. They would, moreover, have clearly stated goals, such as: an enhanced understanding of the manifestations of cultural and institutional racism and their impact in one's own community; the creation of mutually beneficial coalitions across racial lines; and the empowerment of people of color and white allies to effect serious change.

We believe that these organized community dialogues need to be carefully structured, with a clear agenda hammered out in advance by white folks and people of color, and skillfully facilitated to create a level of safety that allows participants to speak openly—on the emotional as well as cognitive levels—without fear of reprisal.

When planning a public forum to discuss racism in one's community, organizers must recognize that people of color and white people do not usually enter the dialogue with the same level of awareness or sophistication about these issues. People of color know a great deal about white America—they must, to function in this country. They also know a great deal about racism. In contrast, much of white America remains remarkably unaware of the lives, feelings, and hardships of people of color.

One of the most common questions asked by whites in our dismantling racism workshops is: What do I call them? Black or African American? Latino/a or Hispanic? Native American or Indian? And so on. Although no longer surprised by this question, we are dismayed by it because it is indicative of the degree of white people's insulation from communities of color.

Many people of color understand the power differential inherent in the three manifestations of racism: personal, cultural, and institutional. They view racism not as an individual issue but as a systemic problem. However, many white people still characterize racism as a virulent form of individual prejudice—they reduce the problem to what Peggy McIntosh calls "individual acts of meanness." They are unschooled in the systematic ways that racism has been institutionalized and are oblivious to the reality of privilege given automatically and invisibly to white people every single day.

Because it is almost inevitable that white people and people of color will begin any discussion of racism with vastly different perceptions of the problem, a public dialogue needs to begin with white people doing something for which they may have little practice: listening intently to people of color. Whites need to listen to the stories and the struggles of people of color in their own or surrounding communities. Not judge, debate, defend, solve, or critique—but listen. Through the simple act of listening, the subtle and pervasive nature of "neoracism"—the racism of the 1980s and 1990s—may become evident.

LISTENING AND BELIEVING

However, listening itself will not reach hearts or change minds unless white people are encouraged to take another step that contradicts countless messages from their growing years, that is: to believe people of color. Although simple, this combination of listening and believing makes for a radical prescription.

Asking white people to listen to and to believe people of color sounds like an easy request. But, in our experience, whites almost invariably resist the idea, and deny that they don't believe people of color. Genuinely believing people of color requires that white people examine some of the messages, images, and cues received as children that taught them otherwise.

Understanding Race Privilege

Although some Black Americans resent it, White Americans have a view on how we can resolve the problem of race. Although some White Americans resent it, Black Americans can challenge us to reflect on our own race. Among other things, that means that we have to recognize that the flip side of racial discrimination is racial privilege, which consists of all those things that come to White Americans in the normal course of living; all the things they take for granted that a Black person must never take for granted. Race privilege is a harder concept to grasp than racial discrimination, especially for Whites, because it is more subtle. It is rooted in assumptions about every day, yet there is no denying it. For example, if I'm looking to buy a house and I'm White, I never fear someone will say no to me because of my race, but if I'm Black, I constantly make assessments about what is possible, problematic or impossible. That freedom from fear is a White skin privilege. If I'm White, I know that if I meet the economic criteria I'll get the loan. If I'm Black, I know I might not. Skin privilege means that I don't have to worry that my behavior will reflect positively or negatively on my race.

Bill Bradley, *Vital Speeches of the Day*, February 1, 1996.

Most white people were not given overt messages in their growing years to doubt people of color, they simply absorbed the prevailing bias in society of white superiority. Consequently, whites learned to "second guess" people of color, to assume they were smarter, and to dismiss information that they heard from people of color that contradicted their own experience in the world. But, with modeling, guidance, and support, whites can be helped to listen with an open mind and an undefended and believing heart. Imagine the difference in our communities if white people started listening intently to people of color and believing that what they were hearing was actually true.

Unfortunately, most people have had few opportunities to witness the kind of open, honest, and mutually respectful dialogue that we envision. They do not know how to begin, are uncertain of how to challenge old behaviors and assumptions, and are afraid to let down their defenses.

We have found that both white people and people of color benefit when community dialogues on racism are cofacilitated by a biracial team willing to engage in frank dialogue between themselves as a model for the group. This modeling provides a concrete example of the level of trust and openness expected in the dialogue, and helps develop a sense of safety in the room.

Public dialogue of this nature seems to work best when people speak from their own experiences about their own lives. If participants make a commitment to an ongoing series of meetings, it is both effective and useful—for the reasons outlined above—to have the people of color speak first about their struggles and tell their stories. We have facilitated gatherings where people of color voluntarily responded to a set of questions presented by the facilitators. This structure gives the discussion a starting point and a sense of boundaries, and brings the dialogue to the personal and community level immediately.

CAUCUS GROUPS

Many people of color are weary of educating white people about racism, and may not want to participate in such forums. People of color should be given full support if they decide that a public community dialogue where they would be speaking about their lives and struggles is not an event they choose to participate in for whatever reasons. The community dialogue should only include those people of color who feel they have something to gain as well as something to give, and who willingly choose to participate.

A helpful exercise that speaks directly to the twin issues of people of color continuously having to educate white folks and white folks often being less informed about race issues is meeting in caucus groups. This exercise involves subdividing by race and having the people of color meet separately with the facilitator of color and the white people meet with the white facilitator.

Caucuses provide folks with a safe place to explore difficult issues with members of their own group. The people of color may focus on empowerment issues and building a strong sense of group solidarity; the white people often struggle with their understanding of racism and how to be effective allies. We have found that, in this arrangement, people raise difficult questions that were previously unasked, members push one another, and confrontation is less threatening than in a racially mixed group. With skillful facilitation, caucus groups can accelerate the changes—greater openness, an ability truly to hear one another, and feelings of empathy—that are necessary for the community dialogue to be effective.

As is evident from our comments thus far, we believe in the

power of modeling as a way to guide people into new behaviors. We have seen the tremendous impact that Cornel West and Michael Lerner have had as they crisscross the country modeling an open, honest, and respectful dialogue on black-Jewish relations. Maya Angelou and Elie Wiesel also share the same stage talking about victimization, empowerment, and building alliances across differences.

We feel that more public dialogues are needed that focus on black-white relations, or more generally, whites and people of color. We have imagined Angela Davis, bell hooks, or Toni Morrison teamed up with Morris Dees, Jimmy Carter, or Bill Bradley to discuss racism in America.

As a biracial team, we have taken part in just such an endeavor, engaging in an exchange we call "Women, Race, and Racism: A Dialogue in Black and White." People have expressed tremendous gratitude that we are able to talk about racism openly from our different perspectives and view this sort of an exchange as a concrete step in the journey toward justice. We encourage other biracial pairs to consider modeling for others a public dialogue about these issues; in our experience, it is an effective way to demonstrate the dialogue we hope to create on the community level.

We need to create public dialogues to move beyond polite and empty words, beyond slogans and accusations, and beyond the fears and hurts that close us off one from another. We must remember, however, that community dialogue is not an end in itself. It is an important and necessary beginning. Our goal is to move people along the continuum from uninformed to informed, from informed to concerned, and from concerned to active.

As a nation, we suffer from what Cornel West has called a "weak will to justice." In our experience, effective community dialogue can be a way both to demonstrate and to strengthen our will to become active in the task of dismantling racism. If we choose to invest the care and the time to organize the dialogue well, and if we decide to speak and to listen in a spirit of openness and trust, we can find avenues to join with one another to confront and dismantle racism in our own communities.

"[The multiculturalists' sensitivity sessions] are a frontal assault on the guiding principles of Western civilization."

DIVERSITY-TRAINING PROGRAMS ARE COUNTERPRODUCTIVE

Nicholas Damask and James Damask

In the following viewpoint, Nicholas Damask and James Damask take issue with supporters of diversity-training programs. In their opinion, multicultural sensitivity sessions are often overly critical of European-based culture and do not promote cross-racial understanding. Citing incidents of bullying, intimidation, public humiliation, and racist indoctrination that have occurred at some diversity-training sessions on a college campus, the authors conclude that such programs do not help to alleviate discrimination. Nicholas Damask is a doctoral student in political science at the University of Cincinnati. James Damask is pursuing a master's degree in business administration at the Heriot-Watt Business School in Edinburgh, Scotland.

As you read, consider the following questions:

1. What are some of the points included in Mary Ellen Ashley's *Nine-Point Plan to Combat Racism*, according to the authors?
2. According to the authors, what kind of experience did "Cheryl" have at Eric Abercrumbie's diversity-training seminar?
3. What is multiculturalism at its core, in the authors' opinion?

From Nicholas Damask and James Damask, "Inside Room 101." This article appeared in the November 1994 issue and is reprinted with permission from the *World & I*, a publication of The Washington Times Corporation, ©1994.

Beethoven was black.

The speaker, a bespectacled black man named Edwin Nichols, noted the German composer's facial features while flipping up a crude sketch. He rummaged through his other sketches.

Blacks know through rhythm.

A nationally prominent lecturer on "diversity in the workplace," Nichols was addressing more than one hundred faculty members from the University College at the University of Cincinnati (U.C.), a state school of thirty-five thousand students in this quiet midwestern city.

Whites are genetically oppressive.

Invited by the college's Committee on Teaching Strategies for the Multicultural Classroom in April 1990, Nichols had flown in from Washington, D.C. It was one of his several appearances at the university.

A young assistant professor ("Professor Taggart"*), new to U.C., also attended this particular session. At one point, Nichols asked all faculty members to stand. He then asked each one to remain standing, based upon where he had received his university degrees. Taggart quickly found herself to be among the last faculty members standing, thereby advertising that she had obtained all her education from prestigious, private universities.

Nichols used the exercise to find an example of what he termed "the privileged white elite." Later attempting to prove Taggart was clearly a member of this elite, he began to comment on her blonde hair and blue eyes. At one point Nichols suggested having a beauty contest, but then sarcastically withdrew his suggestion, noting that everyone would know who would win. Nichols then asked Taggart to stand again—and when she sat frozen in her seat, he embarrassed her to the point that she broke down and sobbed.

A THOUGHT-CONTROL MOVEMENT

Walter Williams, in a February 1993 column, called this and similar incidents on other university campuses part of the political correctness problem. He even likened it to a "Nazi brownshirt thought-control movement."

But within a week of Williams' column in the Cincinnati Enquirer, University of Cincinnati Vice President David Hartleb, in a letter to the editor, explicitly denied that the incident ever took place. Hartleb wrote, "This is a fabricated story. . . . We do not conduct our instructional programs in this way, nor would we

*Names that first appear in quotes have been changed to protect the people involved.

allow a consultant to treat us or our colleagues with intimidation or 'thought control.'. . . This incident never happened.". . .

University Vice President Hartleb in his letter to the Enquirer made it clear that not only was Nichols' character above reproach but that the university "would never allow a consultant to treat us or our colleagues with intimidation or 'thought control.'"

Craig Cobane disagrees. In 1991, Cobane entered a University of Cincinnati graduate program in political science and obtained a job as a residence adviser (R.A.) in the dormitory system. The job and accompanying scholarship allowed him to continue his education, since his father had died several months prior and Craig had given all his life savings to help support his mother and younger sister.

In order to keep his job and scholarship, Cobane attended a mandatory sensitivity training session sponsored by the U.C. Office of Residence Life. Several veteran staff members privately warned Cobane that he should "be careful" in the sessions and "the best thing" would be for him to "keep his mouth shut." Concerned, he approached his supervisor and explained that since his father had just passed away, he simply was not capable of handling an emotional experience. His supervisor attempted to calm Cobane and assuage any fears he might have of the upcoming sensitivity session.

Sensitivity Training?

During the session, the sensitivity trainer divided the R.A.'s into two groups and asked each "to build the tallest structure" with a set of Tinkertoys. Only Cobane and the other white male in his group participated, the women and minorities in the group finding themselves bored with the exercise. In the end, Cobane and his partner built a taller Tinkertoy structure than the one built by the other group, comprised of a mix of race and gender. Cobane flashed a triumphant smile to the other group.

The sensitivity trainer exploded. She accused Cobane of being concerned only with building the taller structure, with competing, with acting selfishly, and with listening only to the other white male. Continuing to attack Cobane, the sensitivity trainer not only called him a racist but also made references to his past, especially about his deceased father, facts she could have known only had Cobane's supervisor informed her. At one point she claimed that "it's not so bad that your father's deceased," because it meant that there was "one less racist influence" in his life. She went on to stress the need to "unteach" all the views his family, and especially his father, had instilled in him.

Cobane is not the only unlucky one. In May 1991, Mary Ellen Ashley, a vice-provost of the university, subjected U.C. library employee William Daniels and others to a mandatory sensitivity session. To evangelize her beliefs, Ashley has written a manual entitled *A Nine-Point Plan to Combat Racism*. Several of the points in her "plan" include ensuring access and retention of minority students; "training" U.C. employees and students in "acceptable social interaction"; developing a "multicultural curriculum"; and setting a timetable for the "elimination [of] racist attitudes, beliefs, and behaviors." To assist in these endeavors, Ashley has formed what she terms a "Racial Incidents Team" for reporting "harassment" on campus.

DIVERSITY PROGRAMS ARE DIVISIVE

The problem with many diversity programs is their inherent divisiveness—a built-in We-They syndrome that pits people against each other. Diversity under these circumstances is not the stuff of brotherly love. It promotes intolerance between groups, making compromise nearly impossible. Group competition can easily deteriorate into a kind of warfare, leaving little more in common than mutual antagonisms and a struggle for spoils.

Lawrence Criner, *Washington Times*, December 14, 1994.

During the session, Ashley stated that "the rules would change" on the university campus, that white males would be expected to participate in diversity and sensitivity sessions instead of sitting quietly during them. Ashley stated that there was, "to put it charitably, a host of ignorance" among the group because nobody in it had read an article in the U.C. alumni magazine that explained her *Nine-Point Plan*. She criticized the U.C. library for not having enough books in the field of cultural diversity even though few people attending the session had any input over such matters. Finally, when a male member of the group stated that he didn't think that he needed sensitivity training, Ashley asked the rest of the group if they could imagine the "gall" it would take to believe such a thing.

U.C. does not limit its sensitivity sessions to just men. Kirsten Swanson, a U.C. alumna, states that she was forced to attend a sensitivity training session in her women's dormitory because a white woman on her floor had *allegedly* made a racial slur to one or more of the black women. During the session (made mandatory for all white women and conducted by the male president of the black student association), the whites on Swanson's floor were "essentially bullied for over an hour" about their alleged racism. Swanson reports that as a result of this horrible experience, the white women on her floor became "paranoid about selecting completely inoffensive words for even the most casual of daily conversations."

PREFERENTIAL TREATMENT FOR MINORITIES

The university's strange notions about "sensitivity" extend to criminal matters on the campus. In February 1993 "Ellis," an R.A., played in a university intramural basketball game with four other white students on his team against a team having among its players two black students (both 250-pound male students). After the game, the two black U.C. students (who apparently did not appreciate losing to whites) assaulted Ellis and his teammates. During the "fight," the two black students kicked and punched Ellis in the face. They even punched the referee, a paid university official, when he tried to break up the fight. To avoid participating in a lengthy criminal trial, the five students filed complaints with the U.C. Office of Residence Life with the understanding that the two black students would be expelled. (One was already on "strict university probation" for thefts and assaults in the dorms, including assaults on other blacks.)

But instead of expelling the students, the U.C. administration asked the five whites to meet with the two black students. During the meeting, the blacks said that they "were just mad" because during the game the white students "were saying stuff" to them. When Ellis made the reasonable point that "saying stuff" does not justify assault, the black students replied that "you gotta understand, this is the way we were brought up."

After the meeting, Ellis' supervisor informed him and the others that "everything's fine now and there's no hard feelings"; the students would not be expelled. The supervisor added that it was the goal of the administration to "help black men to get through college"—presumably even if a few people get assaulted along the way. Ellis explains that "you see things like this every day, and you just kind of have to turn your head." He adds: "There is a system that is set up here at the university, and black people can milk it if they want to. The ones that choose to milk it are set. Even the ones that don't choose to milk it end up getting protected."

BULLYING AND RACIST JOKES

One student's experience eerily resembles Taggart's. In spring 1993, the U.C. Office of Residence Life mandated that all residence advisers attend a series of employee training seminars, including one taught by Eric Abercrumbie, director of U.C.'s Office of Ethnic Programs. The Office of Residence Life emphasized one session more than the others, says "Cheryl," an R.A.: "It was pushed that all Caucasians go" to Abercrumbie's seminar.

At the beginning of the session, it seemed relatively harmless. But midway through it, "something snapped," according to Cheryl, with Abercrumbie pointing her out in the audience and demanding she define terms like *nigger lover* and *oreo*. Abercrumbie challenged another white R.A. in the session to "shake hands like a black guy." The mostly black audience reeled with laughter.

Abercrumbie then probed the white R.A.'s on their education. He asked Cheryl whether any black students had attended her rural, Catholic high school—and nodded knowingly to the audience when she responded that only six or seven black students had been enrolled. Abercrumbie's conclusion: Attending a rural, Catholic school was proof of Cheryl's racism.

Abercrumbie then started questioning her family life, asking Cheryl whether she thought her brother could dance. (Because Cheryl's parents are divorced, she has rarely seen her brother in recent years.) Confused, she sat helplessly as the audience jeered, denying the possibility that her brother could dance as well as a black person. Amid the hoots and catcalls, Cheryl cried. Undaunted, Abercrumbie continued the seminar, making ethnic jokes about whites along the way.

A RACIAL DOUBLE STANDARD

People like Craig, William, Kirsten, and Cheryl have apparently come to understand that it is only by the "sanction of the victim" that the University of Cincinnati can act the way it does. Only by using the students' willingness to be silent can the university continue to sponsor these outrageous sensitivity sessions and allow a racial double standard. Withdraw that sanction, as these students have done by making public these revelations, and it will be difficult for the university to continue its antics. Ellis echoes this sentiment when he angrily states: "I got assaulted almost a year ago, and if I can't talk about that to whoever I want, then how am I supposed to have peace about it? I never got justice for what happened to me. I should be able to tell somebody else about it because they never took care of it."

The multiculturalists assert that their sensitivity sessions are simply a way of achieving "cultural understanding" and "diversity." The sessions are nothing of the sort. They are a frontal assault on the guiding principles of Western civilization: reason and individualism. Indeed, the multiculturalists proudly proclaim that, for example, "logic and objectivity are white male values" and "blacks know through rhythm." At its core, multiculturalism is a mish-mash of racial collectivism, antirationalism, and a mystical faith in the wonders of ethnicity. The sensitivity sessions are simply a crude method of foisting these beliefs on generally captive audiences.

"The notion that differences . . . must be erased for justice and equality to prevail . . . helps keep racist thinking and action intact."

MULTICULTURALISM CAN HELP END DISCRIMINATION

bell hooks

bell hooks is Distinguished Professor of English at City College in New York and the author of *Killing Rage: Ending Racism*, from which the following viewpoint is excerpted. According to hooks, some civil rights advocates believe that society must ignore race, class, and ethnic differences in order to end discrimination. However, hooks asserts, this theory is misguided. The best way to create a nondiscriminatory society, she argues, is to affirm and celebrate the distinctive cultural backgrounds of all races and ethnicities.

As you read, consider the following questions:

1. Why, in hooks's opinion, was Martin Luther King's dream a "flawed vision"?
2. According to the author, why do the supporters of *beloved community* remain committed to ending racism?
3. How do some blacks participate in spreading racism, in hooks's opinion?

S ome days it is just hard to accept that racism can still be such a powerful dominating force in all our lives. When I remember all that black and white folks together have sacrificed to challenge and change white supremacy, when I remember the individuals who gave their lives to the cause of racial justice, my heart is deeply saddened that we have not fulfilled their shared dream of ending racism, of creating a new culture, a place for the beloved community. Early on in his work for civil rights, long before his consciousness had been deeply radicalized by resistance to militarism and global Western imperialism, Martin Luther King imagined a beloved community where race would be transcended, forgotten, where no one would see skin color. This dream has not been realized. From its inception it was a flawed vision. The flaw, however, was not the imagining of a beloved community; it was the insistence that such a community could exist only if we erased and forgot racial difference.

THE STRUGGLE FOR COMMUNITY

Many citizens of these United States still long to live in a society where beloved community can be formed—where loving ties of care and knowing bind us together in our differences. We cannot surrender that longing—if we do we will never see an end to racism. These days it is an untalked-about longing. Most folks in this society have become so cynical about ending racism, so convinced that solidarity across racial differences can never be a reality, that they make no effort to build community. Those of us who are not cynical, who still cherish the vision of beloved community, sustain our conviction that we need such bonding not because we cling to utopian fantasies but because we have struggled all our lives to create this community. In my blackness I have struggled together with white comrades in the segregated South. Sharing that struggle we came to know deeply, intimately, with all our minds and hearts that we can all divest of racism and white supremacy if we so desire. We divest through our commitment to and engagement with anti-racist struggle. Even though that commitment was first made in the mind and heart, it is realized by concrete action, by anti-racist living and being.

Over the years my love and admiration for those black and white southerners in my hometown who worked together to realize racial justice deepens, as does their love of me. We have gone off from that time of legalized segregation to create intimate lives for ourselves that include loving engagement with all races and ethnicities. The small circles of love we have managed to form in our individual lives represent a concrete realistic reminder that *beloved community* is not a dream, that it already exists for those of us who have done the work of educating ourselves for critical consciousness in ways that enabled a letting go of white supremacist assumptions and values. The process of decolonization (unlearning white supremacy by divesting of white privilege if we were white or vestiges of internalized racism if we were black) transformed our minds and our habits of being.

THE AFFIRMATION OF DIFFERENCE

In the segregated South those black and white folks who struggled together for racial justice (many of whom grounded their actions not in radical politics but in religious conviction) were bound by a shared belief in the transformative power of love. Understanding that love was the antithesis of the will to dominate and subjugate, we allowed that longing to know love, to love one another, to radicalize us politically. That love was not sentimental. It did not blind us to the reality that racism was deeply systemic and that only by realizing that love in concrete political actions that might involve sacrifice, even the surrender of one's life, would white supremacy be fundamentally challenged. We knew the sweetness of *beloved community*.

DIVERSITY IS NOT DIVISIVE

Multiculturalism [assumes] that we have no single national identity or belief system but rather a set of diverse and sometimes conflicting identities and beliefs. Our cultural diversity is the result of a common history that we experienced differently. The painful divisions are caused by inequality and oppression, not by the cultural products that give form and voice to the pain and may help us understand one another. Everyone possesses a gender, a race and a class identity, and saying so should not be regarded as sacrilege.

Lillian S. Robinson, *Insight*, July 18, 1994.

What those of us who have not died now know, that generations before us did not grasp, was that *beloved community* is formed not by the eradication of difference but by its affirmation, by each of us claiming the identities and cultural legacies that shape who we are and how we live in the world. To form *beloved community* we do not surrender ties to precious origins. We deepen those bondings by connecting them with an anti-racist struggle which is at heart always a movement to disrupt that clinging to cultural legacies that demands investment in notions of racial purity, authenticity, nationalist fundamentalism. The notion that differences of skin color, class background, and cultural heritage must be erased for justice and equality to prevail is a brand of popular false consciousness that helps keep racist thinking and action intact. Most folks are threatened by the notion that they must give up allegiances to specific cultural legacies in order to have harmony. Such suspicion is healthy. Unfortunately, as long as our society holds up a vision of democracy that requires the surrender of bonds and ties to legacies folks hold dear, challenging racism and white supremacy will seem like an action that diminishes and destabilizes. . . .

INTERNALIZED SUPREMACIST ASSUMPTIONS

More than ever before in our history, black Americans are succumbing to and internalizing the racist assumption that there can be no meaningful bonds of intimacy between blacks and whites. It is fascinating to explore why it is that black people trapped in the worst situation of racial oppression—enslavement—had the foresight to see that it would be disempowering for them to lose sight of the capacity of white people to transform themselves and divest of white supremacy, even as many black folks today who in no way suffer such extreme racist oppression and exploitation are convinced that white people will not repudiate racism. Contemporary black folks, like their white counterparts, have passively accepted the internalization of white supremacist assumptions. Organized white supremacists have always taught that there can never be trust and intimacy between the superior white race and the inferior black race. When black people internalize these sentiments, no resistance to white supremacy is taking place; rather we become complicit in spreading racist notions. It does not matter that so many black people feel white people will never repudiate racism because of being daily assaulted by white denial and refusal of accountability. We must not allow the actions of white folks who blindly endorse racism to determine the direction of our resistance. Like our white allies in struggle we must consistently keep the faith, by always sharing the truth that white people can be anti-racist, that racism is not some immutable character flaw.

Of course many white people are comfortable with a rhetoric of race that suggests racism cannot be changed, that all white people are "inherently racist" simply because they are born and raised in this society. Such misguided thinking socializes white people both to remain ignorant of the way in which white supremacist attitudes are learned and to assume a posture of learned helplessness as though they have no agency—no capacity to resist this thinking. Luckily we have many autobiographies by white folks committed to anti-racist struggle that provide documentary testimony that many of these individuals repudiated racism when they were children. Far from passively accepting it as inherent, they instinctively felt it was wrong. Many of them witnessed bizarre acts of white racist aggression towards black folks in everyday life and responded to the injustice of the situation. Sadly, in our times so many white folks are easily convinced by racist whites and black folks who have internalized racism that they can never be really free of racism. . . .

THE COMMITMENT TO A SHARED VISION

Whites, people of color, and black folks are reluctant to commit themselves fully and deeply to an anti-racist struggle that is ongoing because there is such a pervasive feeling of hopelessness—a conviction that nothing will ever change. How any of us can continue to hold those feelings when we study the history of racism in this society and see how much has changed makes no logical sense. Clearly we have not gone far enough. In the late sixties, Martin Luther King posed the question "Where do we go from here?" To live in anti-racist society we must collectively renew our commitment to a democratic vision of racial justice and equality. Pursuing that vision we create a culture where beloved community flourishes and is sustained. Those of us who know the joy of being with folks from all walks of life, all races, who are fundamentally anti-racist in their habits of being, need to give public testimony. We need to share not only what we have experienced but the conditions of change that make such an experience possible. The interracial circle of love that I know can happen because each individual present in it has made his or her own commitment to living an anti-racist life and to furthering the struggle to end white supremacy will become a reality for everyone only if those of us who have created these communities share how they emerge in our lives and the strategies we use to sustain them. Our devout commitment to building diverse communities is central. These commitments to anti-racist living are just one expression of who we are and what we share with one another but they form the foundation of that sharing. Like all beloved communities we affirm our differences. It is this generous spirit of affirmation that gives us the courage to challenge one another, to work through misunderstandings, especially those that have to do with race and racism. In a beloved community solidarity and trust are grounded in profound commitment to a shared vision. Those of us who are always anti-racist long for a world in which everyone can form a *beloved* community where borders can be crossed and cultural hybridity celebrated. Anyone can begin to make such a community by truly seeking to live in an anti-racist world. If that longing guides our vision and our actions, the new culture will be born and anti-racist communities of resistance will emerge everywhere. That is where we must go from here.

"The melting pot has been replaced
by a mosaic, the separate
components of which regard one
another with apathy or contempt."

MULTICULTURALISM DISCRIMINATES AGAINST WHITES

Lawrence Auster

In the following viewpoint, Lawrence Auster argues that encouraging multiracial diversity harms traditional American culture and the white population. Auster contends that minorities unjustly criticize white American culture, values, and institutions as racist. Efforts to introduce racial diversity into the arts and schools, he asserts, have simply created more tensions between the races. White Americans should abandon attempts at multiculturalism and instead insist that nonwhite minorities accept the historically predominant culture of the nation, Auster concludes. Auster is the author of *The Path to National Suicide: An Essay on Immigration and Multiculturalism*.

As you read, consider the following questions:

1. In Auster's opinion, how do the effects of nonwhite immigration compare with the effects of preferential minority admissions to college?
2. How do developments in the arts illustrate the problems with multicultural populations, according to Auster?
3. In the author's opinion, what truths must Americans recognize to counter the "race-conscious" politics of the United States?

From Lawrence Auster, "Immigration and Multiculturalism," *Culture Wars*, September 1995. Reprinted by permission.

E merging out of the chaos of our time are two bedrock truths about race and race relations that go against everything contemporary Westerners have been taught.

The first truth is that there are significant differences in average intelligence between different populations, and that such gaps in intelligence cannot be closed by any known human means.

The second truth is that not all groups are equally assimilable to each other, in the sense of the ability to come to share a common outlook, identity and way of being. The greater the historical and racial differences between two peoples, and the greater the numbers involved, the harder assimilation is going to be, and the more likely it becomes that conflict between such different peoples will be permanent.

Today's liberal and conservative orthodoxies hold the opposite beliefs—first, that all racial groups are equal in inherent abilities, and second, that all racial groups in the world, no matter how different, are at bottom basically alike and equally assimilable into American culture.

The first belief, in the equality of abilities, leads to the notion that any actual differences in achievement between races must be due to discrimination, which is to be overcome by preferential racial quotas. The second belief, that everyone in the world is equally assimilable, has led to an immigration policy based on what are in effect racial quotas applied to the entire world. The continuing influx of over a million immigrants per year, 90 percent of them non-Europeans, combined with higher nonwhite birth rates, is steadily turning America into a multiracial, nonwhite country—a "mirror" of the entire world.

WHITES AS SCAPEGOATS

A good way to understand the impact of massive nonwhite immigration on American society is to compare it to the impact of preferential minority admissions in the university. As Dinesh D'Souza has described in *Illiberal Education*, universities admit underqualified minority students, while assuring them that they are perfectly well qualified. When these students find themselves having academic difficulties, they blame "institutional racism," then they blame the curriculum itself, which they say is culturally alien to them.

The administration, not wanting to admit the truth, eagerly agrees with the minority activists that there is indeed racism at work. In effect, the administration makes the entire university community, especially the white students and the faculty, the scapegoat for a racial inequality that was created by the administration itself when it admitted unqualified minorities. The school then sets up coercive "anti-racist" programs and speech codes aimed at whites, and adopts multicultural curricula and intellectual standards that conform to minority cultures and "learning styles." When white students protest these things, the minorities, in D'Souza's words, "conclude that they have discovered the latent bigotry for which they have been searching."

In sum, the result of admitting large numbers of unqualified minorities into a university is that whites start to be demonized as racist and are systematically silenced, while their civilizational heritage is attacked as unrepresentative and illegitimate and begins to be systematically dismantled.

Now if all these things happen when you admit large numbers of nonwhite students into a predominantly white school, what happens when you admit massive numbers of nonwhite immigrants into a predominantly white society? The very same things. The failure of the nonwhite population to fit into the society is blamed on the society itself, rather than on the fact that they were admitted in the first place. The white majority starts to be demonized as racist and is systematically silenced, while their civilization is attacked as illegitimate and begins to be systematically dismantled. The great irony is that the admission of nonwhites is supposed to prove that the society is nonracist and egalitarian, yet the more nonwhites are admitted, the more racist and unequal the society seems.

A Troubled Mosaic

While the "delegitimizing" impact of unassimilable immigrants can be seen in many areas of American life, such as education, criminal law, and national identity, in no other field is the problem of unassimilability more obvious than in the arts. Cultural institutions in cities with large Third World populations are rapidly abandoning the Western high culture tradition in favor of Third World folk cultures. According to music critic Edward Rothstein writing in the *New Republic*, the new immigrants simply aren't interested in Western music:

> [S]trikingly in a city like New York, [classical music culture] is largely a racially stratified culture as well: there are almost no black or immigrant faces (aside from Asians) to be seen in concert halls. . . . My neighborhood arts organization, like many others around the country, has been unsuccessful in marketing Western art music to the new racial and international communities in the area. So instead they've begun presenting the folk musics of immigrant and black cultures.

The same applies to the theater. "The reason that Broadway appeals less to New Yorkers these days," writes theater critic Thomas Disch, "isn't just that Broadway has changed: so have New Yorkers. . . . [A] glance around the lobby at any Broadway show reveals who isn't there: any of the city's readily identifiable minorities—black, Hispanics, Asians. . . ."

"It isn't just the expense," Mr. Disch continues, "it's the fact that New Yorkers no longer have a common culture. The melting pot has been replaced by a mosaic, the separate components of which regard one another with apathy or contempt."

Theatrical companies have tried to address the problem by introducing multiracial casts into Western plays, but have been disturbed to find that the audiences for such multiracial productions are still almost exclusively white. Evidently, Third Worlders are simply not attracted to Western theater, even when it has lots of nonwhites in the cast. Since changing the cast doesn't work, the only solution will be to give up the plays themselves.

The irony, once again, is that these problems are not seen as the result of nonwhites' lack of interest in Western culture, and therefore as an indication of their unassimilability; rather, Western culture itself is blamed for not appealing to nonwhites.

Thus the arts institutions of Boston have come under attack because, according to the Boston Globe, the "mainstream cathedral-like halls of Eurocentric culture" do not represent or include "the racial groups that are expected to make up more than 40 percent of the Boston population by the year 2000 and to exceed the white population two or three decades later." Classical ballet, the Globe continues, is now considered a "racist" art form, since it grew out of "white monarchies in Europe," and has historically "excluded" blacks and other minorities. . . .

AMERICAN HERITAGE UNDER ATTACK

Artistic images of American history are also coming under attack. Rush Limbaugh noted in 1994 that the state of Oregon, after commissioning a beautiful bronze statue of a 19th century pioneer family, had rejected the completed work because the image of a white pioneer family was considered "racist" and "non-inclusive." While Rush was unusually upset about this incident, which he saw as an example of political correctness, it didn't seem to occur to him that it had anything to do with demographic change—i.e., that it is our society's increasingly non-white character that is making any "all-white" image seem non-representative and therefore illegitimate.

In 1993 there was an angry protest by black and Hispanic

students at the University of Massachusetts who wanted the school to dump its official symbol, the Minuteman. The image of a "white man carrying a gun," they charged, was racist. For the time being the administration has resisted this demand. But for how long? As the university's white population continues to decline, can we expect the Chinese and Pakistani students of the future to care enough about the image of the Minuteman to defend it against intimidating black and Hispanic protesters? Who will preserve the symbols of our Anglo-European national heritage after whites are gone?

UNDERMINING WESTERN TRADITIONS

What makes multiculturalism a matter for serious concern is its transformation into an extreme ideology whose purpose is to undermine the significance of Western civilization by claiming that Western traditions, because of their pervasive racism, sexism, and elitism, are the cause of most of our modern problems. An increasing number of writers, for example, now believe that considerations of ethnic origin, class, and gender are more important in making policy decisions for arts education than the historical influence or artistic excellence of works of art.

Ralph A. Smith, *Arts Education Policy Review*, March/April 1993.

Indeed, who will defend that heritage even now, while whites are still the majority? In Long Island a 1994 school production of *Peter Pan* was cancelled at the last minute, after six weeks of rehearsals, because the town's American Indian minority felt that the play's portrayal of Indians (which, remember, is simply a childlike fantasy taking place in Never-Never Land) would be insulting to them. So, to accommodate multiracial America, this classic play that we all remember with fondness from our childhood is to be proscribed. The most significant thing about the incident was that no one in the town, including the parents whose children had their play taken away from them, seriously protested this outrage.

In an even more horrifying example of white surrender, an elite private school in New England was considering hiring a well-known multicultural curriculum consultant when it was discovered that the consultant—a Caribbean-born black woman based in Toronto—had admitted in a published interview that her approach would make white children feel intimidated and guilty. After some discussion, the school's board of trustees went ahead and hired her anyway.

I could go on with many more examples, but it's not necessary. The proscription of *Peter Pan*, the hiring of a diversity consultant who announces in advance that she is going to intimidate white children—these are symbols of what is happening to our entire country and culture. As America becomes more and more nonwhite, everything we think of as the American culture and identity will be censored, squeezed out or transformed into something else. . . .

"RACE-NEUTRALITY" IS A WEAPON

What is it that prevents the white majority from protesting its own demographic and cultural dispossession? The most common explanation is that people fear being called racist. That is true, and it's not just political correctness. Deep in the American mind is the ideal of America as a country where advancement is open to anyone, where "it doesn't matter who your parents were." The fatal problem with that formula is that it can only work within certain limits—when you're speaking of individuals sharing a basic commonality. If you apply it *en masse* to radically diverse populations, it becomes absurd and dangerous. The ideal of "race-neutrality," applied to incommensurable groups, turns out to be not race-neutral at all, but becomes a weapon used by one race to dispossess the other.

I came across a remarkable example of this in the coverage of the 1994 South African election. Amidst all the media's joyous talk about a "nonracial" or "multiracial" democracy being born, *Newsweek* came out with a sensational cover with bold letters crying "Black Power!" So deep is the doublethink in which we live today, that I wonder if more than a handful of people noticed the gross contradiction of celebrating black power in what was supposed to be a "nonracial" election. But of course it's not a contradiction at all: What "nonracial" really means is that it is whites who are supposed to be indifferent to race, in order to help nonwhites advance their racial interests.

This same double standard and delusion works across the board. For example, the belief that all the peoples of the world are equal in intellectual abilities is thought to be a race-neutral or "nonracial" idea, since it is saying that race doesn't matter. But since the races are not equal in average abilities, this "nonracial" doctrine of equality turns out to be completely racial. It holds that blacks, on average, have the same abilities as whites, i.e., it holds that blacks have far greater abilities than they in fact have, and invariably blames white racism for the actual failure of blacks to achieve at the same level as whites. It therefore becomes the duty of whites, until the end of time, to exhaust their wealth and spiritual energy in a hopeless effort to make blacks collectively equal to themselves. Meanwhile, black rage at whites for blacks' own failures results in many blacks automatically acquitting black criminal defendants and even justifying racial murder. . . . The "nonracial" belief in equality thus turns out to be the basis of a black racialist mythology that is destroying our society.

Similarly, our immigration policy, which is thought to be race-neutral, is in fact turning America into a nonwhite country, dispossessing white America and its culture. Yet it is considered "racist" to oppose this policy, and "nonracist" to support it. . . .

A RACE-CONSCIOUS POLITICS BASED ON TRUTH

Before we recoil in horror or embarrassment from speaking explicitly about race, let us remember that America's current politics is already a race-conscious politics; only it's a politics based on lies about race; it's a politics directed against whites and their civilization; and it pretends that it's not about race at all, but that it's race-neutral and universal. So instead of today's race-conscious politics, which is based on lies about race, let us have a race-conscious politics based on truths about race.

These truths include the following propositions:

•Long-term harmonious relations between a racial majority and racial minorities are only possible when the minorities do not exceed a certain percentage of the population.

•While individuals of different race living in the same society can get along on a basis of equality and mutual recognition, entire races, living in the same society, cannot.

•In the right circumstances, individuals or small groups of one people can be assimilated into a host culture of a different people; but there are limits to such assimilation. Certainly if the entire people associated with the host culture is displaced or swamped by a different people, the host culture will also disappear. Even smaller numbers can be enough to delegitimize the host culture and produce chronic cultural conflict.

•Therefore, the culture, identity and traditions of white America and Western civilization cannot survive in any community or institution that becomes multiracial and white-minority.

•Because of the greater attractiveness, prosperity and openness of white Western societies, nonwhites will keep moving into them as long as they can. Therefore white America can only survive demographically and culturally if it recognizes itself as a threatened ethnoculture; if it ceases or drastically reduces, on a national scale, all non-European immigration and if it assures, on a local scale, communities where its own institutions may survive. Such local autonomy would require a return to constitutional federalism limiting the power of the central government over local institutions and communities.

•Finally, the large and enduring differences in average intelligence between blacks and whites means that blacks cannot in any foreseeable future be expected to achieve collective economic equality and other kind of parity with whites. The forced attempt to achieve such equality, through affirmative action and through endless attacks on white racism as the supposed cause of actually existing inequalities, can only break down all the institutions and standards of society and lead to race warfare. . . .

It should be understood that the above propositions have nothing to do with race-hatred of the other, or with race-worship of one's own. They are based, rather, on a Christian recognition of our human limitations, namely that we do not possess the godlike power to create a perfect world where everyone is equal and where differences don't matter. If there is any arrogance to be seen today, it is in our current immigration and affirmative action policies, which are among the greatest examples of hubris in the history of the world.

At bottom, this is simply an appeal to justice. The injustice of the current double standard, which advances nonwhites by demeaning whites and dismantling their civilization, is intolerable. And that is why the principles I've described need to be at the center of an anti-multiculturalist, pro-Western civilization politics in this country. In my view, given current demographic realities, any conservative politics that lacks these principles cannot be a serious politics.

PERIODICAL BIBLIOGRAPHY

The following articles have been selected to supplement the diverse views presented in this chapter. Addresses are provided for periodicals not indexed in the *Readers' Guide to Periodical Litera-ture*, the *Alternative Press Index*, the *Social Sciences Index*, or the *Index to Legal Periodicals and Books*.

Eugenie Allen — "Surviving Diversity Training," *Working Woman*, September 1995.

Max Boot — "Oppression Studies Go Corporate," *Wall Street Journal*, August 24, 1994.

Linda Chavez — "Demystifying Multiculturalism," *National Review*, February 21, 1994.

Dissent — "Affirmative Action: A Symposium," Fall 1995.

Peter Duignan — "The Dangers of Multiculturalism," *Vital Speeches of the Day*, June 1, 1995.

Franklin I. Gamwell — "Affirmative Action: Is It Democratic?" *Christian Century*, January 24, 1996.

Vincent J. Genovesi — "Human and Civil Rights for Gays and Lesbians," *America*, April 22, 1995.

Lani Guinier — "Democracy's Conversation," *Nation*, January 23, 1995.

Richard D. Kahlenberg — "Equal Opportunity Critics," *New Republic*, July 17 & 24, 1995.

Charles L. King — "Multiculturalism in Theory and Practice," *Chronicles*, September 1995. Available from the Rockford Institute, 934 N. Main St., Rockford, IL 61103-7061.

Los Angeles Times — "Work Force Diversity: Getting Along and Getting Ahead," May 16, 1994. Available from Reprints, Times Mirror Square, Los Angeles, CA 90053.

Glenn C. Loury — "Individualism Before Multiculturalism," *Public Interest*, Fall 1995.

Arch Puddington — "Will Affirmative Action Survive?" *Commentary*, October 1995.

Joan Walsh — "Can Diversity Training Move Them Up?" *Glamour*, November 1995.

FOR FURTHER DISCUSSION

CHAPTER 1

1. Byron M. Roth argues that the high number of single-parent households among African Americans is the reason for black poverty, while Robert Staples contends that racial discrimination often limits blacks' economic success. What evidence does each author present to support his conclusion? Whose argument is more persuasive? Why?

2. Sandra Lipsitz Bem contends that the workplace does not meet the needs of working women. Warren Farrell argues that men face unrecognized discrimination in the workplace. In each viewpoint, try to find two supporting arguments that you personally agree with. Why do you agree with them?

3. Leslie Marmon Silko argues that the U.S. Border Patrol discriminates against people of color who are U.S. citizens, while William Norman Grigg contends that the Border Patrol is overwhelmed by large numbers of illegal immigrants whose presence threatens America's institutions. What evidence does each author present to support his or her argument? Which author's use of evidence do you find more convincing? Explain.

4. Brian McNaught uses hypothetical examples to support his argument that homophobic and heterosexist attitudes lead to antigay discrimination. Justin Raimondo maintains that homosexuals do not face significant discrimination, using statistics and anecdotal examples to back up his conclusion. Which type of argument do you find more compelling? Why?

CHAPTER 2

1. Joe R. Feagin and Melvin P. Sikes claim that the discrimination blacks often encounter in stores, restaurants, and other public places is rooted in racism. Dinesh D'Souza argues that such discrimination is not necessarily racist but may be based on other factors. How do you think Feagin and Sikes would respond to the distinction D'Souza makes between rational and racist discrimination? Explain your answer, using examples from the viewpoints.

2. Doris Y. Wilkinson argues that desegregated schools do not provide the best learning environments for African American children. She incorporates the opinions of two experienced teachers to support her conclusions. How does her use of personal testimony influence your opinion of her viewpoint? Are

you persuaded by her argument? Why or why not?

3. Raul Yzaguirre and Judy Scales-Trent disagree about the potential effects of a multiracial category in U.S. census population surveys. Do you believe that such a category is necessary? Why or why not? Support your answer with evidence from the viewpoints.

CHAPTER 3

1. Steven Yates argues that affirmative action leads to quotas and reverse discrimination. Nancy Stein and her colleagues take issue with Yates's contentions. In each viewpoint, try to find two supporting arguments with which you agree. Find two with which you disagree.

2. Malik Miah is identified as the managing editor of a socialist newsmagazine. Does this information influence your assessment of his argument that U.S. corporations use racial divisiveness to ensure higher profits? Explain.

3. Rush H. Limbaugh III maintains that "politically correct" attitudes and policies on college campuses victimize conservatives and white males. What examples does he use to support his argument? Does John K. Wilson's viewpoint effectively refute Limbaugh's examples? Why or why not?

CHAPTER 4

1. Ward Connerly and Jamin B. Raskin take opposing positions on the issue of affirmative action in college admissions. Connerly argues that admissions policies should be color-blind and gender-neutral, while Raskin maintains that a student's race and gender should be considered in admissions decisions. Which viewpoint do you agree with, and why?

2. Nicholas Damask and James Damask describe a diversity-training program at the University of Cincinnati that left many white attendees feeling bullied, intimidated, and harassed. What suggestions do you think Andrea Ayvazian and Beverly Daniel Tatum would offer to improve the university's diversity-training program? Do you think these suggestions would be effective? Why or why not?

3. bell hooks argues that whites and people of color can create multicultural communities free from racial discrimination; Lawrence Auster believes that multiculturalism is counterproductive. Compare their opinions, then formulate your own argument about the viability of multiculturalism in American society.

ORGANIZATIONS TO CONTACT

The editors have compiled the following list of organizations concerned with the issues debated in this book. The descriptions are derived from materials provided by the organizations. All have publications or information available for interested readers. The list was compiled on the date of publication of the present volume; names, addresses, phone and fax numbers, and e-mail/Internet addresses may change. Be aware that many organizations take several weeks or longer to respond to inquiries, so allow as much time as possible.

American-Arab Anti-Discrimination Committee (ADC)
4201 Connecticut Ave. NW, Suite 300
Washington, DC 20008
(202) 244-2990
fax: (202) 244-3196
e-mail: adc@adc.org

ADC is a nonsectarian, nonpartisan civil rights organization dedicated to combating discrimination against Arab-Americans and promoting intercultural awareness. It works to protect Arab-American rights through a national network of chapters. The committee publishes the newsletter *ADC Times* ten times a year as well as an annual special report summarizing incidents of hate crimes, discrimination, and defamation against Arab-Americans.

American Civil Liberties Union (ACLU)
132 W. 43rd St.
New York, NY 10036
(212) 944-9800
fax: (212) 869-9065

The ACLU is a national organization that works to defend Americans' civil rights guaranteed by the U.S. Constitution. Its goal is the establishment of equality before the law, regardless of race, color, sexual orientation, or national origin. The ACLU publishes and distributes policy statements, pamphlets, and the semiannual newsletter *Civil Liberties Alert*.

Anti-Defamation League (ADL)
823 United Nations Plaza
New York, NY 10017
(212) 490-2525

The ADL works to stop the defamation of Jews and to ensure fair treatment for all U.S. citizens. Its publications include the periodic *Dimensions* and the quarterly *Facts* magazines.

Cato Institute

1000 Massachusetts Ave. NW
Washington, DC 20001-5403
(202) 842-0200
fax: (202) 842-3490
Internet: http://www.cato.org

The Cato Institute is a libertarian public policy research foundation dedicated to limiting the role of government and protecting individual liberties. It researches claims of discrimination and opposes affirmative action. The institute publishes the quarterly magazine *Regulation*, the bimonthly *Cato Policy Report*, and numerous books.

Center for the Study of Popular Culture

9911 W. Pico Blvd., Suite 1290
Los Angeles, CA 90035
(310) 843-3699
fax: (310) 843-3692
e-mail: 76712.3274@CompuServe.com

The center is a conservative educational and legal-assistance organization that addresses many topics, including political correctness, cultural diversity, and discrimination. Its civil rights project provides legal assistance to citizens challenging affirmative action and promotes equal opportunity for all individuals. The center publishes four magazines: *Heterodoxy*, the *Defender*, the *Report Card*, and *COMINT*.

Clearinghouse on Women's Issues

PO Box 70603
Friendship Heights, MD 20813
(202) 362-3789
fax: (202) 638-2356

The clearinghouse is a national organization that disseminates information on matters concerning women, with particular emphasis on public policies relating to the economic and educational status of women. It publishes the *CWI Newsletter* nine times a year.

Educational Equity Concepts (EEC)

114 E. 32nd St.
New York, NY 10016
(212) 725-1803
fax: (212) 725-0947

EEC is a national organization that creates programs and materials designed to help educators provide bias-free learning environments and activities. Its mission is to decrease discrimination based on gender, race, ethnicity, and disability. Publications and materials available include vocational education videos and issue papers such as "Mixed Messages" and "Including All of Us."

Focus on the Family
8605 Explorer Dr.
Colorado Springs, CO 80920
(719) 531-3400
fax: (719) 548-4525

Focus on the Family is a conservative Christian organization that promotes traditional family values and gender roles. Its publications include the monthly magazine *Focus on the Family* and the report "Setting the Record Straight: What Research Really Says About the Social Consequences of Homosexuality."

The Heritage Foundation
214 Massachusetts Ave. NE
Washington, DC 20002
(202) 546-4400
fax: (202) 546-0904

The foundation is a conservative public policy research institute dedicated to free-market principles, individual liberty, and limited government. It opposes affirmative action and believes that the private sector, not government, should be allowed to ease social problems and to improve the status of women and minorities. The foundation publishes the quarterly journal *Policy Review* and the bimonthly newsletter *Heritage Today* as well as numerous books and papers.

Human Rights and Race Relations Centre
Suite 1506, 141 Adelaide St. West
Toronto, ON M5H 3L5
CANADA
(416) 481-7793
fax: (416) 481-7793

The centre is a registered charity organization that opposes all types of discrimination. It strives to develop a society free of racism where each ethnic group respects the rights of other groups. It recognizes individuals and institutions that excel in the promotion of race relations or that work for the elimination of discrimination. The centre publishes the weekly newspaper *New Canada*.

Lambda Legal Defense and Education Fund
666 Broadway, Suite 1200
New York, NY 10012-2317
(212) 955-8585
fax: (212) 955-2306

Lambda is a public-interest law firm committed to achieving full recognition of the civil rights of lesbians, gay men, and people with HIV/AIDS. The firm addresses a variety of issues, including constitutional law, employment, same-sex marriage rights, domestic-partner benefits, and HIV/AIDS-related discrimination. Its publications include the quarterly *Lambda Update* and the booklets OUT *on the Job, OUT of a Job: A Lawyer's Overview of the Employment Rights of Lesbians and Gay Men* and *Stopping the Anti-Gay Abuse of Students in Public High Schools.*

Men's Defense Association
17854 Lyons St.
Forest Lake, MN 55025-8107
(612) 464-7887
fax: (612) 464-7135

The association promotes equal rights for men and gathers research, compiles statistics, and offers an attorney referral service for male victims of sex discrimination. It publishes the newsmagazine the *Liberator* and the pamphlet *The Men's Manifesto.*

National Association for the Advancement of Colored People (NAACP)
4805 Mt. Hope Dr.
Baltimore, MD 21215-3297
(410) 358-8900
fax: (410) 486-9257

The NAACP is the oldest and largest civil rights organization in the United States. Its principal objective is to ensure the political, educational, social, and economic equality of minorities. It publishes the magazine *Crisis* ten times a year as well as a variety of newsletters, books, and pamphlets.

The National Center for Men (NCM)
PO Box 555
Old Bethpage, NY 11804
(516) 942-2020
fax: (516) 938-7550

NCM's primary goal is to educate the public about the ways men are harmed by sex discrimination. It publishes various reports and articles and the quarterly *Men's Rights Report.*

National Urban League
500 E. 62nd St.
New York, NY 10021
(212) 310-9000
fax: (212) 593-8250

A community service agency, the Urban League aims to eliminate institutional discrimination in the United States. It also provides services for minorities who experience discrimination in employment, housing, welfare, and other areas. The league publishes the quarterly *BEEP Newsletter* and the quarterly newsletter *Urban League News.*

9 to 5 National Association of Working Women
238 W. Wisconsin Ave., Suite 700
Milwaukee, WI 53203
(414) 274-0925
fax: (414) 272-2970

The organization seeks to gain better pay, opportunities for advancement, elimination of sex and race discrimination, and improved working conditions for female office workers. It publishes the 9 to 5 Newsletter five times a year as well as numerous pamphlets.

Southern Poverty Law Center
Teaching Tolerance/Klanwatch
400 Washington Ave.
Montgomery, AL 36104
(334) 264-0286
fax: (334) 264-0629

The center litigates civil cases to protect the civil rights of poor people, regardless of race. The center's Teaching Tolerance Project creates educational materials that promote tolerance and understanding and distributes them free of charge to teachers and principals. The affiliated Klanwatch Project collects data on white supremacist groups. The center publishes numerous books and reports, the monthly Klanwatch Intelligence Report, and the semiannual Teaching Tolerance.

United States Commission on Civil Rights
1121 Vermont Ave. NW
Washington, DC 20425
(202) 376-8177

A fact-finding body, the commission reports directly to Congress and the president on the effectiveness of equal opportunity laws and programs. A catalog of its numerous publications can be obtained from its Publication Management Division.

Wider Opportunities for Women (WOW)
1325 G St. NW, Lower Level
Washington, DC 20005
(202) 638-3143
fax: (202) 638-4885

WOW works to expand employment opportunities for women by overcoming sex-stereotypic education and training, work segregation, and discrimination in employment practices and wages. In addition to pamphlets and fact sheets, WOW publishes the book A More Promising Future: Strategies to Improve the Workplace and the quarterly Women at Work.

BIBLIOGRAPHY OF BOOKS

Theodore W. Allen — *The Invention of the White Race. Vol. 1, Racial Oppression and Social Control.* New York: Routledge, 1994.

David J. Armor — *Forced Justice: School Desegregation and the Law.* New York: Oxford University Press, 1995.

Patricia Aufderheide, ed. — *Beyond PC: Toward a Politics of Understanding.* Saint Paul, MN: Graywolf Press, 1992.

Richard Bernstein — *Dictatorship of Virtue: Multiculturalism and the Battle for America's Future.* New York: Knopf, 1994.

Clint Bolick — *The Affirmative Action Fraud: Can We Restore the American Civil Rights Vision?* Washington, DC: Cato Institute, 1996.

Peter Brimelow — *Alien Nation: Common Sense About America's Immigration Disaster.* New York: Random House, 1995.

Robert D. Bullard, ed. — *Confronting Environmental Racism: Voices from the Grassroots.* Boston: South End Press, 1993.

Anthony Patrick Carnevale and Susan Carol Stone — *The American Mosaic: An In-Depth Report on the Advantage of Diversity in the U.S. Workforce.* New York: McGraw-Hill, 1995.

Stephen L. Carter — *Reflections of an Affirmative Action Baby.* New York: BasicBooks, 1993.

Lynne V. Cheney — *Telling the Truth: Why Our Culture and Our Country Have Stopped Making Sense—and What We Can Do About It.* New York: Simon & Schuster, 1995.

Ellis Cose — *A Man's World: How Real Is Male Privilege—and How High Is Its Price?* New York: HarperCollins, 1995.

Ellis Cose — *The Rage of a Privileged Class.* New York: HarperCollins, 1993.

George E. Curry, ed. — *The Affirmative Action Debate.* Reading, MA: Addison-Wesley, 1996.

Harlon L. Dalton — *Racial Healing: Confronting the Fear Between Blacks and Whites.* New York: Doubleday, 1995.

Gregory Defreitas — *Inequality at Work: Hispanics in the U.S. Labor Force.* New York: Oxford University Press, 1991.

Dinesh D'Souza — *The End of Racism: Principles for a Multiracial Society.* New York: Free Press, 1995.

Lisa Duran et al.	*Immigrant Rights—and Wrongs.* Los Angeles: Labor/Community Strategy Center, 1994.
Terry Eastland	*Ending Affirmative Action: The Case for Colorblind Justice.* New York: HarperCollins, 1996.
Richard A. Epstein	*Forbidden Grounds: The Case Against Employment Discrimination Laws.* Cambridge, MA: Harvard University Press, 1992.
Joe R. Feagin and Hernan Vera	*White Racism: The Basics.* New York: Routledge, 1994.
Nicola Field	*Over the Rainbow: Money, Class, and Homophobia.* London: Pluto Press, 1995.
Claude S. Fischer et al.	*Inequality by Design: Cracking the Bell Curve Myth.* Princeton, NJ: Princeton University Press, 1996.
Kathleen Gerson	*No Man's Land: Men's Changing Commitments to Family and Work.* New York: BasicBooks, 1993.
Todd Gitlin	*The Twilight of Common Dreams: Why America Is Wracked by Culture Wars.* New York: Henry Holt, 1995.
Steven Goldberg	*Why Men Rule: A Theory of Male Dominance.* Chicago: Open Court, 1993.
George Grant and Mark A. Horne	*Legislating Immorality: The Homosexual Movement Comes Out of the Closet.* Franklin, TN: Moody Press and Legacy Communications, 1993.
Steven Gregory and Roger Sanjek, eds.	*Race.* New Brunswick, NJ: Rutgers University Press, 1994.
Lani Guinier	*The Tyranny of the Majority: Fundamental Fairness in Representative Democracy.* New York: Free Press, 1994.
George Henderson	*Cultural Diversity in the Workplace: Issues and Strategies.* Westport, CT: Quorum Books, 1994.
Richard J. Herrnstein and Charles Murray	*The Bell Curve: Intelligence and Class Structure in American Life.* New York: Free Press, 1994.
Herbert Hill and James E. Jones Jr., eds.	*Race in America: The Struggle for Equality.* Madison: University of Wisconsin Press, 1994.
bell hooks	*Outlaw Culture: Resisting Representations.* New York: Routledge, 1994.
Christopher Jencks and Paul E. Peterson, eds.	*The Urban Underclass.* Washington, DC: Brookings Institution, 1991.

Paul Kivel

Uprooting Racism: How White People Can Work for Racial Justice. Philadelphia: New Society Publishers, 1996.

Glenn C. Loury

One by One from the Inside Out: Essays and Reviews on Race and Responsibility in America. New York: Free Press, 1995.

Gordon MacInnes

Wrong for All the Right Reasons: How White Liberals Have Been Undone by Race. New York: New York University Press, 1995.

Coramae Richey Mann

Unequal Justice: A Question of Color. Bloomington: Indiana University Press, 1993.

Tony Marco

Gay Rights: A Public Health Disaster and Civil Wrong. Ft. Lauderdale, FL: Coral Ridge Ministries, 1992.

Douglas S. Massey and Nancy A. Denton

American Apartheid: Segregation and the Making of the Underclass. Cambridge, MA: Harvard University Press, 1993.

Sherri Matteo

American Women in the Nineties: Today's Critical Issues. Boston: Northeastern University Press, 1993.

Nathan McCall

Makes Me Wanna Holler: A Young Black Man in America. New York: Random House, 1994.

Nicolaus Mills, ed.

Debating Affirmative Action: Race, Gender, Ethnicity, and the Politics of Inclusion. New York: Delta Trade Paperbacks, 1994.

Michael Nava and Robert Dawidoff

Created Equal: Why Gay Rights Matter to America. New York: St. Martin's Press, 1994.

Brent A. Nelson

America Balkanized: Immigration's Challenge to Government. Monterey, VA: American Immigration Control Foundation, 1994.

Charles Ogletree et al.

Beyond the Rodney King Story: An Investigation of Police Conduct in Minority Communities. Boston: Northeastern University Press, 1995.

Melvin L. Oliver and Thomas M. Shapiro

Black Wealth / White Wealth: A New Perspective on Racial Inequality. New York: Routledge, 1995.

Gary Orfield, Susan E. Eaton, and the Harvard Project on School Desegregation

Dismantling Desegregation: The Quiet Reversal of Brown v. Board of Education. New York: New Press, 1996.

Paul Craig Roberts and Lawrence M. Stratton

The New Color Line: How Quotas and Privilege Destroy Democracy. Washington, DC: Regnery, 1995.

Robert Royal, ed.	*Reinventing the American People: Unity and Diversity Today.* Grand Rapids, MI: Eerdmans, 1995.
David O. Sacks and Peter A. Thiel	*The Diversity Myth: "Multiculturalism" and the Politics of Intolerance at Stanford.* Oakland, CA: Independent Institute, 1995.
Myra and David Sadker	*Failing at Fairness: How America's Schools Cheat Girls.* New York: Scribner's, 1994.
Judy Scales-Trent	*Notes of a White Black Woman: Race, Color, Community.* University Park: Pennsylvania State University Press, 1995.
Arthur M. Schlesinger Jr.	*The Disuniting of America: Reflections on a Multicultural Society.* New York: Norton, 1992.
Ella Shohat and Robert Stam	*Unthinking Eurocentrism: Multiculturalism and the Media.* New York: Routledge, 1994.
Peter Skerry	*Mexican Americans: The Ambivalent Minority.* New York: Free Press, 1993.
Paul M. Sniderman	*The Scar of Race.* Cambridge, MA: Harvard University Press, Belknap Press, 1993.
Stephen Steinberg	*Turning Back: The Retreat from Racial Justice in American Thought and Policy.* Boston: Beacon Press, 1995.
Ronald T. Takaki	*A Different Mirror: A History of Multicultural America.* Boston: Little, Brown, 1993.
David Thomas	*Not Guilty: The Case in Defense of Men.* New York: William Morrow, 1993.
Barbara Tizard and Ann Phoenix	*Black, White, or Mixed Race? Race and Racism in the Lives of Young People of Mixed Parentage.* New York: Routledge, 1993.
Ethel Tobach and Betty Rosoff, eds.	*Challenging Racism and Sexism: Alternatives to Genetic Explanations.* New York: Feminist Press, 1994.
Michael Tonry	*Malign Neglect: Race, Crime, and Punishment in America.* New York: Oxford University Press, 1995.
Urvashi Vaid	*Virtual Equality: The Mainstreaming of Gay and Lesbian Liberation.* New York: Anchor Books, 1995.
Yehudi O. Webster	*The Racialization of America.* New York: St. Martin's, 1992.
Cornel West	*Race Matters.* Boston: Beacon Press, 1993.
Tom Wicker	*Tragic Failure: Racial Integration in America.* New York: William Morrow, 1996.

Naomi Wolf   *Fire with Fire: The New Female Power and How It Will*
                            Change the 21st Century. New York: Random
                            House, 1993.

Elisabeth Young-Bruehl   *The Anatomy of Prejudices.* Cambridge, MA:
                            Harvard University Press, 1996.

INDEX

DATE DUE
